NEW HAMPSHIRE
Off the Beaten Path

"Barbara and Stillman Rogers take you on an intimate tour of New Hampshire's nooks and crannies. They know and love their state, and it shows in their writing. You'll find something fun to do in every corner of the state, any time of the year."

> —John Pierce, publisher of *The Old Farmer's Almanac* and vice president of Yankee Publishing, Inc.

". . . [the] Rogers offer us a New Hampshire guidebook that will both entertain and inform New Hampshire natives and visitors alike. This book deserves a permanent home in the glove compartment of your car."

> —The Honorable Walter Peterson, former governor of New Hampshire and president of Franklin Pierce College

NEW HAMPSHIRE

Off the Beaten Path™

by

Barbara Radcliffe Rogers
and
Stillman Rogers

A Voyager Book

The Globe Pequot Press

Old Saybrook, Connecticut

Cover illustration of the Carlton Bridge in Swanzey Center by Cathy Johnson

Interior illustrations by Carole Drong

Off the Beaten Path is a trademark of The Globe Pequot Press, Inc.

Library of Congress Cataloging-in-Publication Data

Rogers, Barbara Radcliffe.
  New Hampshire: off the beaten path / by Barbara Radcliffe Rogers and Stillman Rogers. — 1st ed.
      p. cm.
   "A Voyager book."
   Includes index.
   ISBN 1-56440-023-9
   1. New Hampshire—Description and travel—1981- —Guide-books. I. Rogers, Stillman, 1939- . II. Title.
F32.3.R64 1992
917.4204'43—dc20   91-31175
                                                              CIP

Manufactured in the United States of America
First Edition/ Second Printing

To George Radcliffe and Norman Rogers, the fathers who chose New Hampshire as our childhood home, and to James C. Cleveland, who as a U.S. Congressman worked so long and hard to preserve its character and protect its land.

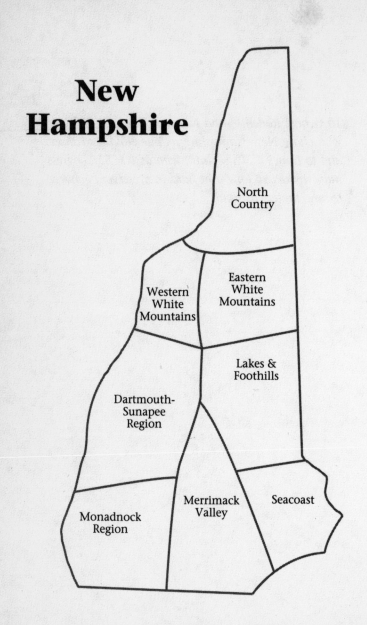

New Hampshire

North Country

Western White Mountains

Eastern White Mountains

Lakes & Foothills

Dartmouth-Sunapee Region

Monadnock Region

Merrimack Valley

Seacoast

Contents

Acknowledgments

Any book is a joint effort, but this one has profited from the help of friends and family all over New Hampshire—and from a number of others who were strangers when we began, but are now counted as friends.

They have shared with us their favorite off the beaten path places, those restaurants, inns, hiking trails, and back roads that even a traveler accustomed to poking into all the corners might miss. Joan Farrel, Carletta Prendergast, Joanne Lemieux, Larry Pletcher, Nina Gardner, Dennis and Sandy Brennan, Dixie Gurian, Philip Hollman, Al Casassa, Philip Mangones, Ron Weeden, Dave Campbell, Mike and Meri Hern, Ray Gorman, and Betty Falton.

Very special thanks go to Len Reed of Bethlehem for the hours he spent telling us about places we would never have found without him. It was Len who also suggested many of the wonderful inns that welcomed us after long days of travel, and which we, in turn, recommend in the book.

We have shared our travels over the years with many friends: hikes and backroads with Patty Hanson, mountain trails and fishing boats with Carol Belsky and John Norton, campfires with Fred and Sta Gursky, and miles of trails above the timberline with Howard and Sue Poore. Possibly the most hilarious of these adventures we have shared with Frank and Maria Sibley, as we searched for gorges, boulders, and ghost towns. Julie and Lura have always been fun to travel with, whether we were slipping over rocky trails in search of a waterfall in a downpour of rain, or enjoying a leisurely second cup of tea at a Portsmouth bakery.

Our fondest appreciation goes to Dee Radcliffe, who has explored every corner of the state and whose notes and suggestions led us to places even the locals didn't know about. Her good humor and enthusiasm will always place her among life's best traveling companions.

Tim and Barbara Rogers

Introduction

How do you introduce a friend, one with whom you've shared many of life's pleasures, one whose company never fails you? What can you possibly say of your friend that will capture those qualities that are most endearing and most enduring?

New Hampshire is that friend to us. The first memories of our childhoods are set here. The first ocean waves we played in broke on New Hampshire beaches; the first mountains we climbed, slopes and trails we skied—they were New Hampshire's. We've lived and traveled in many other parts of the world, but when asked a few days ago which of all the places that we've traveled is our favorite, we said in unison, and without second thought, New Hampshire.

The tremendous diversity of New Hampshire's landscapes makes it visually exciting and also provides a wide variety of activities, particularly for those who enjoy the outdoors. The challenges of its terrain, soil, and climate have given its people a unique character—or perhaps such a place has always attracted those of independent and self-sufficient spirit.

New Hampshire people do tend to be an independent lot; most of them say exactly what they think. Another disconcerting trait to those who don't know us well is that you can't always tell about us by our looks. The size of a person's fortune often bears no relation to the size of one's home or the make of one's car. It is often said of Boston ladies that they don't buy their hats; they *have* them. New Hampshire people are like that too. The beautiful farmhouse may be all that's left several generations later and may be kept up by a lot of hard work alone; the tiny cottage with the gate askew may be the home of a millionaire. We tend to live in what we have.

The same trait is true of restaurants, which is very confusing to the traveler used to decorator interiors and flashy exteriors. You can't always judge a restaurant by its cover, and very often the plainest place or the most staid of inns may have a chef who retired to the country from a four-star bastion of haute cuisine. Surprises are what New Hampshire is full of, and they make each day a happy adventure.

"Off the beaten path" is a relative thing. By most standards, the whole state is off the beaten path. There are only three areas that are congested by traffic even in the height of tourist season. If lodging is heavily booked during the most popular weeks, it is not because there are too many people here, but because resorts do not line our roads. Reservations are always a good idea during July and August and around the first week of October. Some of the places we have chosen for this book are in busy cities but are still little known to visitors. Others are out-of-the-way places in out-of-the-way corners of the state, places such as Garfield Falls that even many local people have not seen. A number of destinations require travel on unpaved roads, but none of these require four-wheel-drive vehicles, except in winter or early spring when some roads are muddy or not plowed and are restricted to traffic.

Which brings us to the question of when to come. New Hampshire is a seasonal state, and each month has its attractions. The best time for you to explore the Granite State depends upon your tastes and interests. Winter is glorious, filled with crystal-cold days for skiing or snowshoeing across white meadows with clear views of mountains through leafless trees. Night brings the stars so close you can spot constellations you never saw before and is a good time for a sleigh ride and a blazing fire in the hearth. Snow covers all the hardscrabble farms and rock-filled fields, and the air is clear and smells of wood smoke. But if you like little museums or want to hike to waterfalls, winter is not the best season.

Spring is good for country walks and hikes. Sugar houses come briefly to life, shrouded in steam and smelling of sweet maple syrup. With the end of the sap run, spring wildflowers carpet the woodlands, and the view of the mountains is softened, but not obscured, by leaves the size of mouse ears. Spring peepers fill the evening air with chirping, and strawberry farms invite you to pick your own. A lot of the little places aren't open yet, but people in the ones that are have time to chat and tell you about local places. Bed and breakfast hosts have time to share a glass of sherry with you after dinner. Spring comes so fast that you can almost watch the apple blossoms unfold.

Summer is full of festivals celebrating almost everything from blueberries to zucchini, and every little town has its historical society open. Days are long and not too hot to enjoy hikes and climbs. Lake shores and mountain brooks offer swimming or just plain cooling off.

After Labor Day, the weather is still summery, but there is a lull in the number of tourists until the end of the month. Farmers' markets are filled with produce and jars of glistening jellies. Hiking is at its very best, and the roadsides are brightened by patches of turning swamp maples.

Foliage paints the state, from north to south, in brilliant shades of red and gold. It begins in mid-September in the north country and lasts until mid- to late October in the Monadnock region. The peak can vary by a week or so, depending on the weather, but any area will have at least two weeks of good color, usually more.

So plan your travel dates according to your own interests and style, or better yet, come often and enjoy the best that each season offers.

Prices are a tricky thing to provide in a guide book, but we have done it anyway. They change with economic conditions, even seasons and weather conditions, since restaurants depend upon the markets for fresh produce and seafood. Lodging rates usually rise during the busiest times and drop during the slower ones. We have given dollar amounts when they seemed fairly likely to remain constant and elsewhere have used general ranges. For bed and breakfast places we consider $60.00 to $70.00 a night for two people to be moderate; for inns and hotels without breakfast, $70.00 to $85.00 is moderate. In restaurants, $10.00 to $20.00 is moderate for the main course, and we've further broken that into a high and low if the prices fall into a close range. How you add to that with other courses and wine will affect your bill, of course, but the entree price sets the base. Sometimes we've been even more specific, especially if the prices are exceptional.

Now to all the usual disclaimers, the caveat emptor endemic to travel guides: Things change, especially in the restaurant business. We've tried to choose places with consistent ownership, but when we discover a great new spot, we can't wait five years to share it with you. If you find our recommendations not up to our descriptions, there are several possible reasons. The restaurant in question may have changed owners or chefs, or it may have just plain gone downhill. Your taste in food may not be the same as ours. One man's pâté is another's "ptoooi," as Confucius wisely observed. There is no substitute for your own good judgment. If you get inside and don't think it's the right place for you, leave. In those memorable cases where a place we've recommended doesn't look like what it tastes like, we've mentioned that fact so that you will expect it. If in doubt, don't be embarrassed to ask to see a menu before you're seated. New Hampshire people don't buy pigs in a poke and they don't expect you to either. Bear this in mind, however: In the last several months of writing this book we have eaten an average of seven meals a week in New Hampshire restaurants. We haven't suggested that you try all of these places, but we never had a terrible meal, and we never had to send anything back to the kitchen. That says a lot about restaurants here.

Enjoy New Hampshire as we do. We think that you'll agree after you've met the state in person that it's a place where familiarity breeds both respect and love.

Off the Beaten Path on the Seacoast

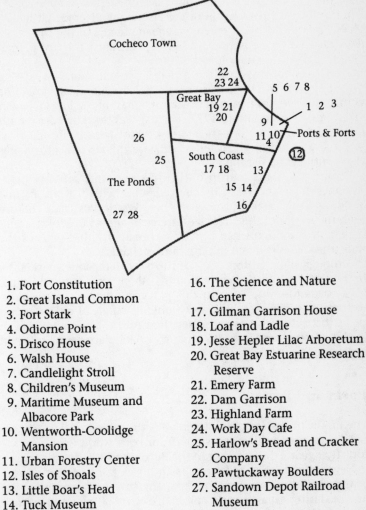

Cocheco Town

22
23 24

Great Bay
19 21
20

5 6 7 8

1 2 3

9
11 10 7 — Ports & Forts
4

26

25

South Coast
17 18   13

The Ponds

15 14

16

27 28

12

1. Fort Constitution
2. Great Island Common
3. Fort Stark
4. Odiorne Point
5. Drisco House
6. Walsh House
7. Candlelight Stroll
8. Children's Museum
9. Maritime Museum and
   Albacore Park
10. Wentworth-Coolidge
    Mansion
11. Urban Forestry Center
12. Isles of Shoals
13. Little Boar's Head
14. Tuck Museum
15. Raspberry Farm

16. The Science and Nature
    Center
17. Gilman Garrison House
18. Loaf and Ladle
19. Jesse Hepler Lilac Arboretum
20. Great Bay Estuarine Research
    Reserve
21. Emery Farm
22. Dam Garrison
23. Highland Farm
24. Work Day Cafe
25. Harlow's Bread and Cracker
    Company
26. Pawtuckaway Boulders
27. Sandown Depot Railroad
    Museum
28. Sandown Meeting House

On The Seacoast

New Hampshire has the shortest seacoast of any coastal state, only 18 miles long, but it's also one of the most historic. The first European settlers established a settlement at Odiorne's Point in 1623, and later the same year a fishing village was established at Dover Point on the northern banks of the Piscataqua River on Little Bay. The Odiorne's Point settlement was abandoned, but the Dover settlers built a meeting house and homes, becoming the first permanent settlement in the colony.

The history of this area, the American colonies, and the young nation are inextricably intertwined. The first American flag to be saluted by a foreign power flew from the mast of the *Ranger,* which sailed from Portsmouth in 1777. The flag was sewn by Portsmouth ladies of fabric cut from their dresses. Portsmouth, for all of its funky shops and bright eateries, still has the air of a prosperous eighteenth-century seaport.

Exeter, too, was a ship-building town and a lively port. Although it has now lost its navigable link with the sea, its fine buildings still speak of the profitable West Indies trade. Inland from the shores of the Great Bay stretched almost unbroken farmland, and, although more heavily settled than other parts of the state, the area is still rich in farms and orchards.

Although most visitors' view of the New Hampshire coast is the traffic and commercialism of Route 1, there are lovely and quiet back roads to enjoy even in this playground area. Portsmouth, too, has its surprises, tucked away amid its tangle of old lanes and paths that turned into streets. New Hampshire, as a colony, began in this seacoast area, and it's an appropriate place for us to begin exploring the state.

Ports and Forts

The link with the sea did not end with the sailing of the last clipper. Ships were built in Portsmouth for both world wars, and the forts that guarded the harbor in the Revolution still dot the coast.

Newcastle, once called Great Island, was the first seat of government and even now looks like the tiny prosperous fishing and seafaring village of its colonial origins. Streets too narrow for sidewalks are lined with houses whose doorways open directly onto the roadway. The numbers on them are not addresses, but dates, most of them from the 1600s and 1700s. It's a place for walking, and the best place to leave your car is **Fort Constitution.**

The fort had its beginning in 1632 with the earthworks and four "great guns"; a blockhouse was built in 1666, and at the end of the century a breastwork was built to protect the military stores. It was named Fort William and Mary.

Paul Revere, the Boston silversmith and patriot, is best known for his ride the night of April 18, 1775. But in New Hampshire, he's remembered for a ride almost four months earlier. On December 13, 1774, he brought a message that British troops were coming from Rhode Island to protect the garrison and secure it against the fractious Sons of Liberty. The next day, four hundred Sons of Liberty converged on the fort and liberated five tons of gunpowder and about one hundred small arms, which they loaded on a gundalow (a type of boat built at Portsmouth and used to navigate tidal rivers) and sailed up the Oyster River to Durham. They hid the gunpowder in a hole under the pulpit of the meetinghouse until they could haul it by ox cart to Cambridge for use at Bunker Hill. On December 15, before the British could get reinforcements, another group helped themselves to sixteen small cannon and whatever other military supplies they could carry off. It was the first active engagement of the Revolution.

Renamed Fort Constitution, it was used in 1812 and every other war until it was returned to the state of New Hampshire in 1961. Its walls and ramparts are a fine place for viewing the lighthouse, harbor, and Fort McNair, which guards the other side of this harbor entrance from Kittery Point, Maine. Be sure to get a copy of the free brochure at the box near the entrance gate. It describes the fort's structure and history. Open 8:00 A.M. to 4:30 P.M. daily.

For access to the rocks and sandy beach of the neighboring shore, go through **Great Island Common,** a park overlooking the harbor. From here you can see two lighthouses, islands, and Fort Constitution, as well as passing sailboats. Rocky tidal areas surround the park with pools to explore and a gentler tide than the one that crashes against the rocks along the ocean. While the beach isn't very long, it's set in a very attractive cove. The park provides picnic tables, a pavilion, and grills, as well as playgrounds, ballfields, and restrooms. There are no camping facilities. Open daily May to September until dark; admission is $2.00 per adult.

Close to this park, look for the entrance to Wild Rose Lane, which ends at **Fort Stark.** It is another of the seven forts built to protect Portsmouth Harbor and the naval shipyard. Although it was the site of earthworks during the Revolution and the War of 1812 and of a later stone fort, the present batteries were built at the turn of the century and were used in both world wars. Be careful as you climb around the batteries; a flashlight will be handy if you plan to explore inside. Look for the tracks in the ceiling of Battery Hunter where ammunition was moved from the magazine and hoisted through a hole in the ceiling to the enormous guns in their emplacements above. The huge steel doors of the magazines stand ajar, grass grows from the cement, and one round gun emplacement has begun to slide down the crumbling cliff. Open Saturday and Sunday 10:00 A.M. to 5:00 P.M. between Memorial Day and Labor Day.

Crossing the bridge to Rye, on the mainland, look for The Ice House, a small carry-out restaurant with picnic tables in an adjoining pine grove. Serving fried clams, fish, and fries, it's a local favorite for inexpensive lunches (603–431–3086). Close by, BG's Restaurant has a dining room overlooking the harbor. Although it looks more like a fisherman's shack, the decor improves inside. The menu offers lobster and seafood at inexpensive to moderate prices. For dinner or lunch call (603) 431–1074.

Facing Newcastle Island and Fort Stark is **Odiorne Point**, where the first Europeans in the state settled. Site of Fort Dearborn during World War II, the grass-covered hills are actually camouflaged bunkers for gun emplacements and their support systems. The entire point is now a nature center, with diverse coastal habitats to explore. Along with the rocky shore and salt marsh, there are a freshwater marsh and coastal woods. A drowned forest of pine, birch, and hemlock stumps is firmly rooted about two feet below tide level at the south end. Throughout the natural habitat you can see signs of human habitation as well. Stone walls of old farmlands and a colony of summer cottages cross the area, and you may see the hardy remnants of some of the formal gardens of the long-gone cottages. The only one of these now standing is the science center. Programs and tours on such varied subjects as wild shore edibles, sea legends, coastal defenses, whales, marshes, and geology are conducted by the New Hampshire Audubon Society and the University of New Hampshire Marine Science Program. Open daily, mid-May to mid-October, 8:00 A.M. to 8:00 P.M. A small entry fee is charged. Write P.O. Box 304, Rye 03870 or call (603) 436–8043 (off-season 603–862–3460). For information on special programs call (603) 862–1088.

Portsmouth is a lively city with warrens of back streets to explore. The path to its abundant historic homes is so well-beaten that a red line is painted on the sidewalks indicating "The Portsmouth Trail." But these are not the only interesting or historic places to visit in Portsmouth.

The original name for the settlement here was Strawbery Banke, after the river banks red with the fruit in the late spring. A restoration preserving nearly four centuries of this old waterfront neighborhood, saved from demolition in the 1950s, now uses the name Strawbery Banke. Thirty of the thirty-five historic homes here stand on their original foundations. The unusual feature of the restoration is that instead of returning the neighborhood to any single period and showing what things looked like then, the buildings and their furnishings show the evolution of homes, gardens, shops, and daily life throughout the entire period of its existence.

The most dramatic example of this whole-history approach is at the **Drisco House,** built in 1795. The house changed with the times, and when it was acquired, one side of the duplex was a "frozen in time" 1950s apartment. It has been saved as it stood, but the other half of the house has been restored to its origins as the store and home of an eighteenth-century mid-level tradesman. This, too, is unusual, for the homes that are usually saved and restored are those of wealthy and prominent citizens—homes far more elegant and ornate than the Drisco House. This one building, with its 1795 and 1955 halves, spans the history of the Puddle Dock neighborhood in Portsmouth.

The process of discovery and restoration is a continuing one, and visitors are invited to share in it through a number of exhibits showing cut-away walls and structural details. The Joshua Jackson and Sherburn houses are dedicated entirely to old house archeology, showing not only how the homes were built, but also how historians can tell the changes made over the centuries. To anyone restoring an older home, looking inside the mechanics of original and renovated construction is an invaluable lesson. To the more casual visitor, it's just plain interesting.

The **Walsh House** shows changing tastes and styles in a different way. The interior of the house was completed in about 1800 by a ship's captain whose tastes were influenced by the changing tastes of the times but rooted in Yankee conservatism. His house was among the first in Portsmouth to use such trendy techniques as faux marble, painted wood graining, arched windows, and a curved stairwell. No two rooms have matching woodwork, and, in some cases, doors joining the rooms have a different construction on each side. Some of the features of the house, such as the painted wood detail on the woodwork and the home's separate dining room, were considered quite avant garde in the North. As a tour guide once described it, "If *Better Homes and Gardens* had been publishing in 1800, they would have featured this house!"

The style and the character of the owners of the Goodwin Mansion are equally evident. For over fifty years the family of a New Hampshire governor of the Civil War era lived here, and his wife's detailed and spirited diaries provide details that have made it possible to restore not only the house, but her remarkable gardens as well. At various times in the summer and fall, Victorian teas are served in the gardens.

The miracle of Strawbery Banke is that all of the restoration and maintenance has been done without the major foundation funding enjoyed by other historic villages of its magnitude. Projects are completed as funds are available, usually from local donations or entry fees. It is exciting to watch the restorations take place, and each visit gives a dimension of being part of its progress. Even the gifts purchased at the Dunaway Store, the museum's shop (and a treasure trove of unusual things not found in other such emporia), help fund the restoration. It's like giving twice when you do your Christmas shopping there.

Speaking of Christmas, on the first two weekends of December, the village opens for a **Candlelight Stroll.** Candles light the windows as you wander through the streets with costumed carolers and musicians. The houses are decorated for the holidays and offer free refreshments to visitors. Craftspeople are at work, and you can shop for gifts in their workshops or in the museum stores. Each year brings new features, and it's an occasion for local people to enjoy the uncrowded winter quiet of Strawbery Banke. The stroll takes place on four evenings only, from 4:30 to 8:30 P.M., and costs $8.00 for adults and $4.00 for children ten to sixteen (younger children are admitted free).

The restored buildings are open daily 10:00 A.M. to 5:00 P.M. from May 1 through October 31. Admission is $9.00 for adults, $8.00 for seniors, $5.00 for ages six to seventeen, and free for children under age six. Write Strawbery Banke, Marcy Street, P.O. Box 300, Portsmouth 03802 or call (603) 433–1100.

Gardeners should stop at Prescott Park across the street to see the All America Show Garden display gardens where they grow each year's All America selections. Show gardens such as this are located in different parts of the country to demonstrate which flowers perform best in various climates. Northerners who spotted boxwood at Strawbery Banke may have wondered how it grows in New Hampshire. The answer is that Portsmouth and a tiny coastal strip are in a different gardening zone from the rest of the state, due to the moderating effect of the sea.

Not just another place to stow the kids on a rainy day, the **Children's Museum** offers discovery adventures in science, history, and the arts all packaged in just plain fun. The Yellow Submarine is at the museum's core, and kids just keep coming back to it. Seeing is not believing at Outta Sight, and a full television studio gives everyone a chance to star in a show while their friends watch it on the screen. Toddlers to teens will love this upbeat center where exhibits change as fast as kids turned loose in the museum's costume trunk. Plan at least an afternoon or even a day here. Take a good book or just watch the fun. Children over nine do not have to be accompanied by an adult. The museum's shop is full of games, books, crafts, and science toys. Both the shop and the recycling center are open without museum admission. Open Tuesday to Saturday 10:00 A.M. to 5:00 P.M. and open Monday during summer and school vacation weeks. Children and adults $3.50, seniors $3.00. Write the museum at 280 Marcy Street, Portsmouth 03801 or call (603) 436–3853.

After the kids explore the Yellow Submarine, you can explore the real thing at the **Maritime Museum and Albacore Park.** Built at the Portsmouth Naval Shipyard in 1953, the *Albacore* never went to war. Her mission was an experimental one, as she was planned to be redesigned and adapted as the prototype for the submarine of the future. The teardrop hull design made her the fastest submarine ever put in the water. That and dive brakes, sonar systems, and other new theories tested on board have become part of modern submarine design. The fascinating story of this experimental submarine and how its fifty-five-member crew lived in its 205-foot by 27-foot confines during its nineteen years of commission is told during a ten-minute video and a half-hour tour of the vessel. Now sunk in a dry basin so you can see the

Children's Museum, Portsmouth

entire hull, the USS *Albacore* looks a bit like a beached whale up close. It's the only one of its kind, so if the sea and its ships interest you at all, don't pass up the chance to see it. Open 9:30 A.M. to 4:30 P.M. every day; the last tour begins at 4:00 P.M. Adults $4.00, seniors $3.00, children seven to twelve $2.00, families $10.00. You'll find the *Albacore* on the Market Street Extension, or Route 1 bypass. Write P.O. Box 4367, Portsmouth 03801 or call (603) 436–3680.

With all of the things to do in Portsmouth, you are sure to be looking for a place to eat by now. There are plenty to choose from, since downtown Portsmouth has more restaurants in a smaller area than any other part of New Hampshire. Everyone has a few favorites, so we'll tell you ours. The Bagelry at 19 Market Street has outstanding breakfast bagels and lunch or snack sandwiches (603–431–5853). The Stock Pot at 53 Bow Street is first choice in good weather for its terrace overlooking the colorful, busy harbor, not to mention its inexpensive, hearty soups, sandwiches, and full dinners (603–431–1851). The Ceres Bakery, at 51 Penhallow Street, bakes incomparable breads, cookies, tortes, and coffee cakes. Nowhere else will you find such generous slices of the last two served up for $1.00 to $1.50. Hearty thick soups are served with a slice of their daily bread, or you can choose from two quiches or several salads. A good lunch here with dessert will be under $5.00. It opens at 5:30 A.M. for travelers who like to be on the road early (603–431–6518). For those who prefer a hearty breakfast "at home," the Inn at Christian Shore is a bed and breakfast in a restored Federal home on Maplewood Avenue (603–431–6770).

Out of town, where the Little Harbor Road ends at the water's edge, is the **Wentworth-Coolidge Mansion.** It is one of very few residences of a royal governor virtually unchanged since the Revolution. The governor lived well. The home that he built in 1750 was originally even larger and was the most elegant of its day. It was not only his residence, but the center of government as well, and you can tour the original rooms and the Governor's Council Chamber, where he signed the charters for land grants and towns throughout New Hampshire and Vermont. The grounds, where you are welcome to picnic, are planted in the first lilacs brought to the New World. They are the state flower, and if you visit the state in May you will see them blooming in dooryards, gardens, and at the sites of long-deserted farms throughout the countryside. Although technically an "exotic" here, lilacs have

9

a long history in the state and have been accepted as a native. Open from 10:00 A.M. to 5:00 P.M. from Memorial Day to Labor Day. (Perhaps this is a good place to mention that Memorial Day in New Hampshire is still observed on May 30, not the nearest Monday.) The Wentworth-Coolidge Mansion is on Little Harbor Road, off Route 1A in Portsmouth (603–436–6607).

South of Portsmouth, not far from Route 1, is the 150-acre property of the **Urban Forestry Center.** Not just a beautiful place to visit for its gardens, woodland, and salt marsh landscapes, it is an attractive demonstration area whose purpose is not only to protect this piece of land, but also to show others how they can protect and enhance their own property. Individuals, municipalities, developers, and conservation commissions all look to the center for inspiration and advice. Throughout the property are mailboxes where you will find extensive information on each project. At the raised vegetable garden bed, for example, is free information on building the beds, choosing the soil, composting, cold frames, pest control, and succession crops. Plant-by-plant descriptions are available at the perennial border, and a thorough booklet on herb culture and uses, prepared by Tanya Jackson (one of New England's leading herb experts), is free at the herb garden.

A "Garden for the Senses," created especially for the visually and physically impaired, emphasizes plants selected for flavor, fragrance, color, and texture. Wide paths and raised beds give easy access. A fitness trail with exercise stations encourages multiple uses of the property. A tree identification trail, arboretum, fire ecology study area, and several plantations, as well as ample area for observing birds that live in the marsh and shore areas, add to the center's attractions. Free and open year-round, the trails are favorites of cross-country skiers and snowshoe hikers (no motorized recreational vehicles). The center is at 45 Elwyn Road (off Lafayette Road) in Portsmouth; call (603) 431–6774 for more information.

Off the coast, shared with Maine, but with access from New Hampshire, and visible only in clear weather, are the **Isles of Shoals.** Described by the writer and poet Celia Thaxter, who grew up there, they were painted by the Impressionist painter Childe Hassam, who came to the summer arts colony that developed there. His work includes over 400 paintings of the islands, many of which were done to illustrate Thaxter's *An Island Garden,* a classic of garden writing as fresh in its facsimile reprint as it was at its original printing at the turn of the century (see book list, p. 138). These islands are as wrapped in tales of shipwrecks, pirates, ghosts, and buried treasure as they are in fog. Craggy and barren as they were when Captain John Smith called them "barren piles of rock," the islands still fascinate visitors. The Isles of Shoals Steamship Company at 315 Market Street will take passengers to Star Island for a three-hour shore visit. Write them at P.O. Box 311, Portsmouth 03801 or call (603) 431–5500. Whale watching, fishing, harbor, and Great Bay cruises out of Portsmouth are also offered by Portsmouth Harbor Cruises at 64 Ceres Street (603–436–8084).

The South Coast

Boat trips from Rye Harbor are conducted by New Hampshire Seacoast Cruises (603–964–5545) and the Atlantic Fishing Fleet (603–964–5220). For a shorebound excursion that gives you nature on one side and human nature on the other, walk or bicycle around **Little Boar's Head.** A 2-mile path goes along the ridge of a rocky promontory, with waves crashing on the rocks below. Inland stands a row of beach "cottages" built in the pre-income tax days when wealthy city dwellers moved their families and household staffs to the shore for the summer. In the early summer wild roses bloom along the path.

The town of Hampton lies inland, out of hearing distance of raucous Hampton Beach. Follow Park Avenue east from Route 1 to find the original settlement at Meetinghouse Green. The old common is now a memorial park to the first settlers, with a stone for each of the pioneer families put there by their descendants. Across the street is the **Tuck Museum,** operated by the Hampton Historical Society, a group of buildings that includes an old one-room schoolhouse, a museum of early farm implements, the Seacoast Fire Museum, and a variety of exhibits on the area's history. It isn't the Smithsonian but is a very approachable collection; most items are not in glass cases but right where you can see them. A playground on the shady lawn outside will amuse the children if your attention span exceeds theirs. Open 1:00 to 4:00 P.M. Tuesday to Friday from mid-June to mid-September. The museum is at 40 Park Avenue, Hampton 03842; call (603) 926–5510.

On Route 84 in Hampton Falls is the **Raspberry Farm,** where you can pick a quart or two of sweet juicy berries in a few minutes from vines trellised to protect your arms from bramble scratches. You can also buy berries already picked or cooked into delectable jams and jellies. There is always freshly-churned homemade raspberry ice cream in the freezer, as tempting as the fresh berries themselves. Open throughout the summer and into October, noon to 5:00 P.M. Monday to Friday and 9:00 A.M. to 5:00 P.M. Saturday and Sunday. Call (603) 926–6604 for more information.

The Science and Nature Center at New Hampshire Yankee, the area's power station, explores the various sources of energy and their effects on the environment. Hands-on exhibits, such as a bicycle-powered generator (how long can you keep the light burning?) and computerized quizzes, fill the science center, and an aquarium shows local marine life. The Oascoag nature trail winds through woods and marshlands where markers explain the habitats, natural history, and plant life. Shorebirds abound, and muskrats, foxes, rabbits, and woodchucks may wander within sight if you are quiet. Such salt marshes are important sources of food and breeding grounds for wildlife, as well as providing filtration areas to keep groundwater pure. Open Mondays through Saturdays, except holidays, 9:00 A.M. to 4:00 P.M. Closed Saturdays in the winter; free admission. Write Seabrook Station, Route 1, Seabrook 03874 or call (603) 474–9521 or (800) 338–7482.

Exeter, like Portsmouth, is a nice place for walking. Fine homes line its streets, and three of the finest Federal mansions face the bandstand in the center of town. The **Gilman Garrison House** was built of massive hewn logs in the late 1600s as a fortified garrison. In the mid-1700s the house was enlarged and remodeled, adding a wing and more formal rooms in which its owner felt more comfortable entertaining John Wentworth, the royal governor, during his visits to Exeter. These visits ended abruptly when the governor had to take refuge in Fort William and Mary and finally flee altogether at the outbreak of the Revolution. (Since Portsmouth was considered a hotbed of Toryism, the seat of the state's government moved to Exeter—making it the state's first capital.) Later, Daniel Webster boarded in this house while he was a student at Phillips Exeter Academy. Open June 1 to October 1, Tuesday, Thursday, Saturday, and Sunday, noon to 5:00 P.M. The Gilman Garrison House is at the corner of Water and Clifford streets in Exeter; call (603) 436–3205.

The Exeter Handkerchief Company, well known to local quilters and dressmakers, is a treasure house of fabrics and sewing supplies at bargain prices. They have particularly large selections of decorator fabrics and fabrics for bridal and formal wear. Whatever sewing project you're undertaking, someone there will be an expert at it. The Exeter Handkerchief Company is at 48 Lincoln Street in Exeter (603–778–8564).

For an inexpensive meal in Exeter, prepared from healthy fresh ingredients, stop at the **Loaf and Ladle.** Don't look for much atmosphere in this plain, pine-paneled dining room, although in nice weather you can eat on the shaded back porch overlooking the falls. The salad bar is a bargain at $2.25 for a small bowl; you can choose from all the usual vegetables and greens, plus marinated artichoke hearts, feta cheese, and other less common additions. Half sandwiches are generous and are made with a variety of breads, including cardamom and sourdough. Thick hearty homemade soups are their specialty. The Loaf and Ladle is on Water Street; call (603) 778–8955.

Great Bay

Past Portsmouth harbor, the Piscataqua River opens into Little Bay, which is fed by the Oyster River and Great Bay. At 5 miles long, Great Bay is the largest inland body of salt water in New England, but it's very hard to see since only one road, Route 4, passes within sight. Even that allows views of only the northern end. The towns that lie along the rivers feeding it are all far from its tidal shores.

The Lamprey River provided power for the mills at Newmarket, located at the falls. There is now a fish ladder at these falls, just above the mill buildings. On Sunday mornings from 7:30 A.M. until noon, Great Hill Maples serves pancakes featuring their own maple syrup. It is located off Route 108, north of Newmarket.

Durham is best known for the University of New Hampshire, which dominates the town and brings it to life. On part of the campus is a lovely ravine filled with wildflowers in the spring. The **Jesse Hepler Lilac Arboretum** at Nesmith Hall contains a collection of different varieties of the state flower. Open Monday through Friday, 9:00 A.M. to 4:30 P.M.; call (603) 862–3205. At the far end of the campus, a little railroad station is now the UNH Dairy Bar, run by the school of agriculture. It serves the best ice cream in the area (some say in the world) in prodigious quantities. Young's Restaurant, in the center of town, run by the same family for thirty years, makes its own doughnuts.

Hard to find, even by asking passersby, is the **Great Bay Estuarine Research Reserve.** Land access to the more than four thousand acres of tidal waters, mud flats, salt marsh, tidal creek woodlands, fields, and meadows is from Adams Point. There is no nature center or organized visitor program here, but the habitat is filled with the flora and fauna peculiar to tidal estuaries. For a closer look and better understanding of the wildlife that makes its home in the Oyster River Valley and Great Bay, read *A World Alive* by New Hampshire's naturalists laureate, Lorus and Margerie Milne of Durham (see book list, p. 138). Their almost lyrical description of the forces that shaped New Hampshire's landscape is not limited to the confines of the valley of the Oyster River. The action of the glaciers they so clearly describe formed the geographical features we shall explore throughout the state. For information on the Great Bay Reserve, call (603) 868–1095.

Emery Farm was established in 1655, which, eleven generations later, makes it high on the list of the nation's oldest family farms. Here you can pick your own strawberries, blueberries, or raspberries. Juicy tree-ripened peaches and garden produce as well as local maple syrup, honey, and fresh home-baked breads are sold; New Hampshire crafts and pottery add to their unique farmstand. In the spring they sell herb plants and garden flats from their greenhouse. The farm is open every day, Easter through October, 8:00 A.M. to 7:00 P.M., and October through Christmas Eve (they also have Christmas trees) from 9:00 A.M. to 6:00 P.M. Emery Farm is on Route 4, east of Durham (603–742–8495).

Cocheco Town

Dover was the scene of repeated Indian attacks during the early years of the settlement, so nearly all of its garrison houses were destroyed. The only one still surviving is the **Dam Garrison,** which is protected by a roofed lattice portico between two brick buildings of the Woodman Institute. In original condition, this heavy log structure houses a collection of early furnishings and implements. The other two buildings of this privately endowed museum contain historical and natural history exhibits, including a particularly good collection of rocks and minerals. Open Tuesday through Saturday, 2:00 to 5:00 P.M., at The Woodman Institute, 182 Central Avenue, Dover 03820.

A short distance south of The Woodman Institute is the Dover Friends Meeting House, a large wooden building constructed in 1768 at Dover Point. Quakers once made up one third of Dover's population, and meetings are still held there on Sunday mornings at 10:30 A.M.

Salmon Falls Stoneware is a potters' studio where they make salt-glazed stoneware and decorate it by hand with traditional designs. It is open daily, 9:00 A.M. to 5:00 P.M. You can find Salmon Falls Stoneware on Oak Street in Dover (603–749–1467).

Dover is a good place to use as a base while visiting the seacoast area. Quieter than Portsmouth or the beach towns, it is easier to find lodging here, especially in the summer. On UNH graduation day, late in May, however, it is nearly impossible to find lodging within many miles of Dover and Durham, so be sure to call early for reservations if you plan to visit then.

Highland Farm is a gracious bed and breakfast in a large mid-nineteenth-century brick home set in seventy-five acres of river-side meadow. Rooms are bright and large with either queen-sized or double beds and are reached from a broad central hallway and an elegant double staircase. Breakfast, served in a formal dining room, features fresh fruit and homemade muffins or scones in addition to the main dish. The setting is so quiet and lovely that it's tempting to forget sightseeing entirely and enjoy the walking or cross-country ski trails along the river, the gardens, badminton and lawn games, or the hammock on the wide porch shaded by the mulberry tree full of birds. Write Highland Farm, 148 County Farm Road, Dover 03820 or call (603) 743–3399.

Dover doesn't have nearly the assortment of restaurants that Portsmouth does, but **Work Day Cafe** serves a very good selection of Louisiana, Tex-Mex, and Mexican dishes with an original flair. This is not the drowned-in-cheese-and-run-under-the-broiler variety of Mexican. Portions are generous, and there is no shortage of shrimp or andouille sausage in the gumbo or chicken in the flautas. It's a busy, popular place with a fairly young clientele. Prices are inexpensive, particularly when you consider the size of the servings. Work Day Cafe is at Upper Square, Dover; call (603) 749–0483.

For breakfast, everyone goes to Jakes, on Third Street. But expect to stand in line between 6:30 and 8:30 A.M.—it's that popular. Prices are low, and the old-favorite breakfast dishes are prepared just right.

Calef's Country Store, at the crossroads of Routes 9 and 125 in Barrington, is a local institution. Aged cheddar cheese is their specialty, or you can buy real cured or sour dills from the barrel, pickled limes, smoked hams and bacon, soldier beans, or molasses hand cranked from a barrel. Open daily 8:00 A.M. to 6:00 P.M.; write P.O. Box 57, Barrington 03825 or call (603) 664–2231.

The Ponds

After buying traditional cheese at Calef's, you can buy not-so-traditional crackers at **Harlow's Bread and Cracker Company** down Route 125 in Epping. Try samples of the unusual varieties—pizza, spiced, cracked pepper, to name a few—before buying. Their breads are specially delicious, and you can assemble a fine picnic with their creamy quiches, calzones, or delicate foccacio. Don't leave without one of their enormous 50-cent fig bars. These are like nothing that ever came out of a box, and we'll promise you'll go back for more. This unusual bakery is on Route 27, but within sight of the crossroads with Route 125.

With the picnic basket freshly stocked from Harlow's, your next stop should be Pawtuckaway State Park. Along with its picnic area, this large park has both boat and canoe launch areas on the lake, two campgrounds with tent sites, a beach, and several hiking trails. One of these leads to the **Pawtuckaway Boulders,** a field of huge glacial erratics that were broken from the cliffs on the two small mountains nearby and carried by the glacier to their present location a few thousand feet away in a valley to the east. The boulders vary in size, with some as long as 60 feet and over 30 feet high. Paths also lead to the summits of the three small mountains, two of which offer open views to the south. The tallest of these mountains is barely 1,000 feet, so the climbs are short ones. Trails in the park are used for cross-country skiing in the winter. The campgrounds are open from late May to Columbus Day, and reservations are not accepted. Write Pawtuckaway State Park, RFD #1, Raymond 03077; call (603) 895–3301.

The **Sandown Depot Railroad Museum** is housed in a restored 1873 railroad station. It is thought to have been the busiest single-line railroad line in the country, with eighteen freight and sixteen passenger trains passing through Sandown each day. Most of the original railroad equipment is still in place, including the telegraph office. Open June through October, Saturday and Sunday, 1:00 to 5:00 P.M. Admission is free. The museum is on Route 121A in Sandown; call (603) 887–4621 for more information.

Inquire at the museum to see if the **Sandown Meeting House** is open to visitors. Built in 1773 and 1774, it is the finest and best-preserved church structure in the state. It still has its original hand-wrought hinges and latches on the paneled doors, as well as the square pews and slave gallery. (It surprises many to learn that owning slaves was a fairly common practice among wealthier New England families—although never to the extent of the South.) The pulpit is goblet shaped, with a canopy which acts as a sounding board. If you are interested in early construction techniques, ask to see the loft, reached by a ladder from the gallery. Cross beams are staggered, and mortised joints are held by wooden keys. According to a local tale the church took longer to construct than was anticipated and the rum supply ran out. The workmen refused to continue until the supply was replenished.

Off the Beaten Path in the Merrimack Valley

1. America's Stonehenge
2. Robert Frost Homestead
3. Taylor Up and Down Sawmill
4. Chester Village Cemetery
5. Lawrence L. Lee Scouting Museum
6. Manchester Historical Association
7. Red Arrow Lunch
8. Sainte Marie's Church
9. Bedford Village Inn
10. Public archery ranges
11. New Hampshire Historical Society
12. Kimball-Jenkins Estate
13. The Glory of India
14. Silk Farm Wildlife Sanctuary
15. The Yorkshire Rose Tea Shoppe
16. Conservation Center
17. Shaker Village
18. Tilton Arch
19. The Black Swan
20. Martha Wetherbee's Basket Shop
21. Fragrance Shop
22. Mary Saltmarsh Studio
23. Pat's Peak
24. The Bakery
25. Colby Hill Inn
26. Frye's Measure Mill
27. Impressions Pottery

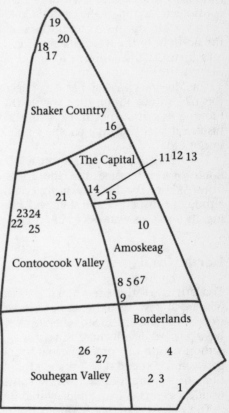

The Merrimack Valley

While the seaport provided the early links that built Portsmouth and Exeter, the size and force of the Merrimack River as it gathered waters from rivers and mountain streams in the north provided power for manufacturing that built the valley cities. Towns sprang up around the mills, and they continued to grow together. Manchester, the state's largest city, grew with the largest cotton-mill complex ever built. Even today, long after the mighty Amoskeag mills closed their doors, the remaining mill buildings continue to dominate the city's riverbank.

This swath up the center of the state is flatter than the land to the north or to the west, characterized by rolling hills, small lakes, and a surprising amount of open space, especially north of Manchester.

The Merrimack Valley has never been tourist country. Most visitors pass through it on their way to the pleasures of the lakes and mountains farther north. Concord is occasionally visited for its historical sites, but Manchester's rich ethnic cultures are largely unnoticed.

The back roads of the Merrimack Valley are worth exploring: Route 28 as it bypasses the cities to its west and Route 13 on the other side of the river. Farming communities dot this road, for although this part of the state was heavily linked to manufacturing, its lowlands were once almost entirely cleared for agriculture.

Borderlands

The origins of the site known as **America's Stonehenge** are obscure at best. Its old name of Mystery Hill is far more accurate since it is quite unlike Stonehenge. Archeologists and astronomers have puzzled over its megaliths, stone chambers, and artifacts, but carbon dating on some charcoal found here indicates an age of between 3,000 and 4,000 years. Monoliths mark the sunset positions of the summer and winter solstices as well as other astronomical events, making it likely that it was a calendrical site.

The place is fascinating, even if you do have to overlook the hokey names such as "Sacrificial Table" and "Oracle Chamber." Unfortunately, much of the site was destroyed by previous owners of the property who sold many of the stones for paving stones and disrupted the arrangement of the stones with a bulldozer. Who carved and moved the stones and built the chambers, as well as when and why and how, is a puzzle that may never be solved, but that mystery makes the place even more fun to visit and explore. Don't expect anything like Stonehenge, however. Open weekends April through November, 10:00 A.M. to 3:30 P.M.; daily May and September, 10:00 A.M. to 4:00 P.M.; and daily June to Labor Day, 9:00 A.M. to 5:00 P.M. Admission is $5.00 for adults, $4.00 for seniors, $3.00 for children ages thirteen to seventeen, and $1.50 for children ages two to six. Follow signs from Route 11, east of Route 28. Write P.O. Box 84, North Salem 03073; call (603) 893–8900 or 432–2530.

The **Robert Frost Homestead** was the home of the poet for the first decade of this century. Frost credited the years that he spent at this Derry farm with shaping his future by providing him

Robert Frost Homestead, Derry

with time and seclusion. The simple 1880s farmhouse, the barn, the brook, orchards, and stone walls mentioned in his poems are all here, much as they were during his time. A nature trail labeled with lines of his poetry winds through meadow and forest. Open daily mid-June to Labor Day and weekends only Memorial Day to mid-June and Labor Day to Columbus Day. The homestead is on Route 28 in Derry (603–432–3091).

Although sawmills are not rare in New Hampshire, the **Taylor Up and Down Sawmill** is the only up-and-down mill still operating. It is water-powered, with gears made of wood. The mill runs on Saturdays in July and August and four other days; you should call for dates if you are interested in seeing it. Write the mill at Ballard State Forest, Island Pond Road, Derry 03038 or call (603) 271–3457.

The **Chester Village Cemetery** dates from 1751 and contains monuments by a number of master colonial stonecarvers. Look especially at the faces of the angels, a common motif on tombstones of the period. The story is that stoneworker Abel Webster, who lived in Chester in the 1700s, had a running theological quarrel with the townspeople, and to get even with them he put frowns on the faces of all the angels on the tombstones. At the crossroads of Routes 121 and 102 in Chester.

If you long for a quiet game of croquet, visit the grass courts of the Hampstead Croquet Association. Stillmeadow Bed and Breakfast on Main Street is within strolling distance, a moderately priced lodging in a pleasantly restored 1850s home. Write P.O. Box 565, Hampstead 03841 or call (603) 329–8381.

Amoskeag

Scouts and leaders will want to stop on the way into Manchester at one of the finest collections of Boy Scout memorabilia and books in the United States. The **Lawrence L. Lee Scouting Museum** is at the headquarters of the Daniel Webster Council, where there are also picnic tables and camping facilities. Open daily in July and August, Saturdays only, September through June on Bodwell Road in Manchester; call (603) 669–8919 for more information.

Although it's hard to miss the red-brick factory buildings that run the length of Manchester, you should visit the **Manchester**

Historical Association for a closer view of how these mills shaped life here. Upstairs in this old-fashioned museum is a room devoted to the mills, where you can see a four-panel photograph of them—it took four shots to get the whole length, and even then it only includes the half that stood on the east side of the river. Fifteen thousand five hundred people worked there. Look through the other exhibits upstairs—a case of clothing and accessories for "Commodore Nutt," the 3-foot-tall star of P.T. Barnum's show, who was born on South Willow Street in the 1840s, and a fully furnished Victorian parlor are among them—before going down two flights to the basement. (The light switch is to your right at the bottom of the stairs.) A scale model of the Amoskeag covered bridge that connected the east and west mills across the river until 1921 takes nearly half of one room, which it shares with a fire wagon and firehouse signs. The earliest Indian relics found in New Hampshire, dating from the paleolithic era, are also down here. All three floors constitute a homey collection displayed in old-fashioned cases without the glamour of modern museum format, but it's just right for the subjects. The museum itself is a period piece, and it will tell you a lot about this hardworking city's blue-collar, down-to-earth history. There is a tiny gift shop on the first floor. The museum is free and nobody bothers you as you browse about, but your contribution will be appreciated even if there is no one to see you put it in the box. Open Tuesday through Friday, 9:00 A.M. to 4:00 P.M. and Saturday, 10:00 A.M. to 4:00 P.M. You'll find it at 129 Amherst Street, Manchester; call (603) 622–7531.

While you're in the frame of mind for down-to-earth, no-frills things, walk a couple of blocks to the **Red Arrow Lunch.** It will be open, whatever the time of day; it has been since 1903. Three booths and a long counter are the capacity of this eatery, and the menu includes stuffed cabbage, chicken pot pie, liver and onions, meat loaf, hot turkey sandwich, chicken parmesan, fried chicken, ham and beans, macaroni and cheese, American chop suey, stuffed peppers—you get the idea. The most expensive entree (which includes vegetables, potatoes, bread, etc.) is the New England boiled dinner at $5.75. Nothing else is over $4.00. On a frosty Sunday night when no one else is open, they'll brew up a separate pot of decaf just for one freezing customer. The waitress will tell you right off that the stuffed cabbages are great tonight, but the meat loaf isn't as good as usual.

Breakfasts are as generous as dinner and just as inexpensive. You might not choose this for your wedding anniversary, but you'll never leave hungry or broke! Open twenty-four hours, seven days a week, all year, at 61 Lowell Avenue (between Chestnut and Elm streets) in Manchester (603–624–2221).

Manchester has a lot of little places to eat, many of them real ethnic restaurants run by people who came from the country whose cuisine is featured. The Athens, on Central Street (603–623–9317), is good for Greek food. The New Canton Take-Out has been preparing Chinese specialties (customers stand at the counter watching the crisp, fresh snow peas come from the refrigerator to the wok) for ten years. Open Monday through Thursday, 11:00 A.M. to 10:30 P.M., Friday, until 11:30 P.M., Sunday, 12:00 noon to 10:00 P.M. It's located at 383 Kelley Street (on the west side) in Manchester (603–668–8477).

Ethnic food markets are found in neighborhoods throughout the city, especially in the streets to the east of Elm Street. Yee's Oriental Market is at 123 Hanover Street (603–668–3362), and Bakolas Market, carrying Greek groceries, is at 110 Spruce Street (603–669–2941). Descendants of both Greek and Polish families in Manchester have maintained strong social and cultural ties, centered on their churches. Each sponsors fairs, bazaars, and cultural events featuring traditional foods and arts. Holy Trinity Polish National Catholic Church is at 635 Union Street (603–622–4524) and Assumption Greek Orthodox Church is at 222 Cedar Street (603–623–2045).

The French-Canadian influence is still strong, with a daily French-language newspaper and the Association Canado-Americaine at 52 Concord Street (603–625–8577), whose library of over four thousand volumes centers on the development of French culture in North America. The west side of town, across the river, was the French-Canadian neighborhood, dominated by the impressive **Sainte Marie's Church.** The architecture is distinctive, and the towering interior is reminiscent of the cathedrals of Quebec and Montreal. Highly ornate, it features statuary, a marble altar, carved woodwork, and a two-tiered gallery. It is so acoustically exact that the New Hampshire Symphony Orchestra and Chorus performs its choral concerts there, featuring such works as the Verdi and Berlioz requiems.

Other musical and performing arts are performed regularly at The Palace Theater, 80 Hanover Street (603–668–5588), while the

Currier Gallery of Art, 120 Orange Street, maintains an outstanding fine and decorative arts collection (603–669–6144).

A few miles west of Manchester in the village of Bedford is the **Bedford Village Inn.** The historic farmhouse is now the restaurant, and the massive barn has been converted into twelve guest suites and two apartments. The central area of the three-story barn has been left open, its post and beam construction clearly visible. Guest rooms open onto a corridor along one side. Luxury is the keynote of the inn: King-sized four-poster beds, full-sized desks, marble bathrooms, whirlpool baths, full-sized sitting rooms, a mixture of antique and reproduction furniture, and individually decorated rooms give it style and comfort. It is not a quaint old inn, but a small modern luxury hotel in an old setting. It's a pleasant combination. At $93.00 for a standard suite, it is among the more expensive lodgings that we recommend. It's also a lot for the money.

The original farmhouse has been left much as it was, its moderate-sized rooms made into small dining rooms. Not only does this make it quieter, but it makes it more personal. A large dining room has been added at the back, glass-enclosed to look out over the garden, arbor, and barn. Again, this makes for an attractive blend of old and new. The proof of any restaurant, however, is in the menu. This one may include sauté of chicken with shallots and raspberry, veal liver with green peppercorns, or scallops and mussels tossed with plum tomato, basil, and a julienne of vegetables. A separate "New Option Menu" offers dishes low in sodium, cholesterol, and fat, but high in flavor. The chicken breast parmesan is baked, pork tenderloin is grilled and served with a roasted pepper puree, and eggless linguine is tossed with sweet peppers and poached salmon. The inn's luncheon menu features dishes such as grilled chicken with pesto, a 3-inch-deep quiche with chunks of lobster, or mixed grill with marinated vegetables. Prices are in the moderate range with several of the "New Option" dinner entrees priced under $10.00. Open daily 11:30 A.M. to 2:00 P.M. for lunch, 5:30 to 8:30 P.M. for dinner, except Sunday, 3:00 to 8:00 P.M. Write The Bedford Village Inn, Old Bedford Road, Bedford 03102. You can call the inn at (603) 472–2602 and the restaurant at 472–2001.

The only **public archery ranges** in New Hampshire are at Bear Brook State Park, northeast of Manchester. Maintained by the Fish and Game Department, each consists of fifteen targets. An additional four-target practice range is wheelchair accessible. The park includes several ponds, two marshes, and a wildlife refuge as well as offering swimming, tent camping, and fishing. Hiking trails cover the area, many of which become cross-country trails in the winter.

One of the very few Civilian Conservation Corps (CCC) camps left in the northeast is in Bear Brook Park. The park's visitor center is in the headquarters building, and the barracks are used for various other purposes. Much of the park land itself was part of the CCC camp during the 1930s, and many of the picnic sites, hiking trails, recreation buildings, and roads you will enjoy on New Hampshire's public lands were built by the CCC. Write Bear Brook State Park, Allenstown 03275 or call (603) 485–9874.

The Capital

Although it is important as the center of government for the state, Concord is not among New Hampshire's largest cities. (Incidentally, if you want to immediately label yourself as an outlander, pronounce *Concord* as you would the usual noun. In New England, it's pronounced "conquered.") Its manufacturing remained small, and it retains even now the appearance of a stately turn-of-the-century city, with its brick business blocks and government buildings of gray granite.

Blending into these buildings that surround the statehouse, and so often overlooked among them that they have hung a colorful banner in front of its columned granite facade, is the **New Hampshire Historical Society.** The sculpture above the entrance is the work of Daniel Chester French, creator of the *Minuteman* statue in Concord, Massachusetts, and the seated Lincoln in Washington, D.C. The collections of the society on permanent display include outstanding examples of New Hampshire furniture and decorative arts. Special exhibits may feature any aspect of New Hampshire history—a term not limited here, as it is so often, to events of previous centuries. These may cover the Shakers, baseball, textile arts, or the life and times of a citizen, famous or little known.

The focal point is an original Concord Coach. Splendid in decorative detail, these coaches were as strong and as well constructed as they were beautiful. They were, in fact, so perfect in their design that from the 1820s to the early 1900s, during which time over three thousand of them were built in Concord, almost no changes were made in their construction. It was the most perfect traveling vehicle known to its times. Wells, Fargo and Company used them, as did most of the other overland dispatch companies. They have often been called "the coach that won the West," but they were also shipped to South Africa, Australia, and South America. You may see them elsewhere in the state—the oldest known to exist is at the Corner Store in Moultonborough. The Concord Coach Society (18 Park Street, Concord 03301) has information on the history and known location of all coaches existing today and works for their preservation and restoration.

The small museum shop in the historical society is an excellent source of publications on New Hampshire and its history. Many of these are privately printed and hard to find elsewhere. They also carry small gifts and historical games and pastimes for children. Open Monday to Friday, 9:00 A.M. to 4:30 P.M. and Saturday and Sunday, noon to 4:30 P.M. The New Hampshire Historical Society is at 30 Park Street in Concord; call (603) 225–3381.

Also on Park Street, right opposite the statehouse, is the Upham-Walker House, largely unchanged since its construction in 1831 and furnished with a number of original pieces. It's open, free of charge, Monday through Friday, 9:00 A.M. to noon and 1:00 to 4:00 P.M.

Completely different in style and architecture from this refined and classic home, the **Kimball-Jenkins Estate** is the epitome of Victorian. Eleven-foot ceilings, hand-carved oak woodwork, and the air of a well-run turn-of-the-century household characterize this home, which stands today exactly as it looked when it was the home of the Kimball family. The grounds that surround it are landscaped in period gardens. Tours of the house end with a proper Victorian tea. Tours by appointment. The Kimball-Jenkins Estate is at 266 North Main Street in Concord; call (603) 225–3932.

A few blocks north of the Kimball-Jenkins Estate, in a plain storefront building, is **The Glory of India.** Authentic Indian food is all they serve, and they do it very well. You can watch the chef at work over the tandoor (a deep Indian oven) through a window in the dining room wall, where you can also look into their spotless kitchen. Begin a meal with a hot coconut soup garnished with pistachios and a sampler plate of appetizers that include crisp samosas and delicate vegetable fritters. Order a lightly seasoned rice to accompany the rich dark sauces, hearty enough to stand up on a fork. You'll find none of the turmeric yellow of boxed curry powder blends, but individually prepared blends of spices and herbs for each dish. Choose mild, medium, or hot sauces according to your taste; the hot is hot, no doubt about it, but not so hot you can't taste the food it accompanies. The menu describes each dish, so you can make educated choices. Chicken, lamb, pork, and fish and shrimp are roasted in the tandoor, as are a wide variety of breads. Some of the breads are filled with herbs, vegetables, and meats, good with a plate of salad for lunch. The dining room is square and plain, with red table linens; it's not a glamorous, exotic setting, but it bespeaks the attitude of these serious young chefs toward the food they serve. Bring your own wine or beer (try New Hampshire's own Frank Jones Ale, brewed just across the river in Pembroke, especially good with curry), or accompany your dinner with the restaurant's own iced tea. Prices are inexpensive to moderate, and entrees are brought on serving dishes, as in Chinese restaurants, so you can share and sample several dishes. Indian food is an acquired taste, and this is an excellent place to acquire it. The Glory of India is at 170 North State Street in Concord; call (603) 228–1628. (The restaurant has easy handicapped accessibility.)

At the other end of Concord is the **Silk Farm Wildlife Sanctuary** and the headquarters of the New Hampshire Audubon Society. Trails traverse the forests and wetlands along the edge of Great Turkey Pond, orchards, hedgerows, and fields where visitors can see rare wildflowers as well as birds and small animals. Audubon House provides a year-round bird blind, an excellent wildlife library, and a shop featuring a variety of nature guides, bird feeders, seed, minerals, and gifts with a wildlife theme. It is open Monday through Saturday, 9:00 A.M. to 5:00 P.M., and Sunday, 1:00 to 5:00 P.M. The library is open Thursday and Saturday, 10:00 A.M. to 4:00 P.M. The New Hampshire Audubon Society is at 3 Silk Farm Road (off Clinton Street) in Concord; call (603) 224–9909 for more information.

Adjoining the sanctuary is St. Paul's School, which owns much of the land upon which the sanctuary lies. Silk Farm Road leads into the back entrance of the St. Paul's campus. The chapel of this private preparatory school has a finely executed fresco in the oratory to the left of its entrance, a replica of Lorenzetti's great fresco at Assisi. Two mobiles by Alexander Calder are also on the campus; one is suspended from the ceiling in the lobby of Memorial Hall, and the other one is on the grounds nearby. The outdoor mobile is stored from November through March to protect it from the harsh winter weather.

A small, but very attractive, bed and breakfast nearby offers moderately priced rooms with private bath. Breakfasts are served overlooking the well-tended grounds of an avid gardener. Pancakes are the house specialty, but all you have to do is ask for your favorite morning dish. Within a short walk are the fine Victorian neighborhoods of "the hill", where restored homes and mansions line the tree-shaded School and Centre streets and the adjoining area. The bed and breakfast is not in a restored historic home, but comfort and hospitality are timeless. Write Charles and Harriet Ward, 43 North Fruit Street, Concord 03301 or call (603) 224–2620.

An unexpected Union Jack hangs over the sidewalk on Main Street to announce the **Yorkshire Rose English Tea Shoppe.** British friends and Anglophiles are right at home in this simply decorated authentic tea room, where Cathryn Crotty has reconstructed a bit of her homeland.

The scones are outstanding (we like the lemon ginger ones). A full afternoon tea includes two of them, plus tea sandwiches— cheddar and chutney, salmon and cucumber—and tea biscuits served on a traditional three-tiered tray. A lunch menu offers Cornish pasties, steak and kidney pie, Sussex sausage roll, and a variety of savory meat pastries. A ploughman's lunch is a plate of bread, English cheeses, and fruit.

A small selection of gifts and foods from the British Isles lines one wall: teas, lemon curd, shortbread, preserves, tinned tea biscuits, toffee, and tea cosies. If you are traveling alone, this is a comfortable place, where you are likely to see others enjoying their china pot of tea over a good book. Conversation is low, and an air of gentility prevails. The Yorkshire Rose is at 8 South Main Street (near its intersection with Pleasant Street) and is open every day, except Sunday, from 11 A.M. to 5 P.M.; call (603) 229–0089.

Across the river to the east, in Concord Heights, the Society for the Protection of New Hampshire Forests' **Conservation Center** maintains several buildings powered by alternative energy sources, as well as nature trails. This organization is responsible for the preservation of huge tracts of land throughout the state by either outright ownership, purchase of development rights, or helping private and governmental bodies in their efforts to save important lands and forests. You can tour their passive-solar building Monday through Friday, 9:00 A.M. to 5:00 P.M., free of charge. There is also a gift shop featuring environmental gifts and publications. Take East Side Drive (Route 132) north from Bridge Street (Route 9) to a left turn onto Portsmouth Street (you will pass the other end of this street going to the right shortly before the turn you want). The address is 54 Portsmouth Street (603–224–9945).

Shaker Country

East Side Drive becomes Mountain Road, still Route 132, which leads to Canterbury and the beautifully maintained **Shaker Village.** Set on a hill among rolling meadows, this was once a thriving 4,000-acre farm where 300 Shakers lived and worshiped in an atmosphere of common ownership, celibacy, and a strong work ethic. Shaker crafts are still admired for their simple design and fine workmanship. In the twenty-two buildings of the village you will see original examples of these in the furnishings of the houses. Skilled craftspeople are at work with wood, fiber, and plants creating baskets, boxes, furniture, rugs, brooms, and herbal crafts. Authentic lunches and dinners are recreated in the Creamery, where they use herbs from the village's garden. Guided tours begin on the hour and take about ninety minutes. Thomas Merton once observed, "The peculiar grace of a Shaker chair is due to the fact that it was built by someone capable of believing that an angel might come and sit on it." Both that grace and its spiritual origins are evident throughout the village. Open May through December, 10:00 A.M. to 5:00 P.M. Admission is $6.75 for adults and $3.50 for children ages six to twelve. Write Canterbury Shaker Village, 288 Shaker Road, Canterbury 03224 or call (603) 783–9511.

The town of Tilton is inextricably linked with the Tilton family, who were the generous benefactors of much of its artistic heritage. Charles Tilton, like many cultured men of his times, believed in the importance of public statuary and began to set about ornamenting his home town with sculpture. Overlooking the town from a steep hillside on the opposite side of the river is the **Tilton Arch,** an exact replica of the Arch of Titus in Rome. Built of Concord granite, it rises 55 feet from its base, upon which lies a red granite lion. It is actually in the town of Northfield, across the

Tilton Arch, Tilton

river, and you can get there via the bridge at the monument on Main Street, turning left on the far side, and going uphill to the Northfield Town Hall. Beside it, a dirt road leads to the top of the hill and the monument.

Some of the smaller of Charles Tilton's statues are gone now, but five of them remain. A marble allegorical statue of America—depicted as an Indian princess—stands on Main Street, as do another of Europa and one of Asia. A zinc statue of Chief Squamtum now stands in a parking lot. An iron footbridge connects the town with an island, once the site of the Tilton summer house and now a shaded park.

Fine mansions still grace Tilton, and two of them, within a stone's throw of each other on West Main Street, are of particular interest. **The Black Swan** bed and breakfast is a beautiful preserved Victorian, filled with period architectural and decorative detail. One guest room includes a huge semicircular sitting room alcove with stained-glass panels over each of its seven windows. Each room has some distinctive antique feature or furnishing, and the dining room is fully paneled in oak with built-in china cupboards and a fireplace. The Victorian parlor is available for use by the guests, as is a refrigerator full of soft drinks. The gardens and lawns sweep down to the banks of the river, overhung by shade trees. It's a thoroughly enjoyable resting place at moderate prices. Write The Black Swan at 308 West Main Street, Tilton 03276; call (603) 286–4524.

Just up the street at 321 West Main Street, Le Chalet Rouge serves memorable French cuisine to a maximum of twenty guests. The menu changes frequently but always includes a selection of classics such as trout amandine, steak au poivre, lamb with rosemary, or roast duck and first courses including pâté, escargots, and smoked trout or mussels. It's in the high moderate range at $14.00 to $18.50 for main course selections, but worth it. Open Tuesday through Saturday from 6:00 P.M.; not all credit cards are accepted. Since seating is limited, you should make reservations (603–286–4035.

A number of fine craftspeople have studios in or near Tilton. **Martha Wetherbee's Basket Shop** has a wide reputation among the Shaker museums throughout the country, for whom she makes reproduction Shaker ash splint baskets. Open Monday through Friday, 9:00 A.M. to 4:00 P.M., all through the year and Saturdays from mid-June to mid-September. The shop is on Eastman Hill Road (off Hermit Hill Road) in Sanbornton (603–286–8927).

The Country Braid House is both a workshop and a showroom for hand-braided wool rugs. Open Monday through Saturday, 9:00 A.M. to 4:00 P.M., on Clark Road in Tilton 03276 (603–286–4511).

Contoocook Valley

West of Concord lies an area of rolling farmlands and attractive villages. Hopkinton's wide Main Street is lined with trees and a number of homes of the colonial era. In the center of town on Main Street is the headquarters of the New Hampshire Antiquarian Society with a museum of early items. Open Monday and Wednesday, 9:00 A.M. to 5:00 P.M., and Monday, 6:00 to 8:00 P.M. (603–746–3825).

To see herbs and perennial flowers in an impressive garden setting, visit the **Fragrance Shop,** where you'll find 150 varieties of field-grown plants for sale. A walk in their gardens is pure joy, and the eighteenth-century barn is filled with wreaths, herb crafts, dried flowers, potpourri, and culinary herb blends as well as garden accessories, such as sundials and bee skeps. Open mid-April through December, Tuesday through Saturday, 10:00 A.M. to 5:00 P.M., on College Hill Road in Hopkinton (603–746–4431).

Mary Saltmarsh Studio preserves the beauty of a spring or summer garden forever (or at least for a long time) inside botanical lampshades. When the light glows through the muslin background, the flowers take on a misty glow of color. Other crafts using dried or pressed herbs and flowers make the workshop seem more like a garden. Open by appointment, on Pine Street in Contoocook (603–746–3873).

The only Henniker on earth was named for a London merchant who was a friend of Royal Governor Benning Wentworth. New England College is in the center of town and gives it a lively air and a series of cross-country ski trails named for Marx Brothers movies. The toughest, which goes over a small mountain, is called "You Bet Your Life."

Skiing is not a newcomer to Henniker. For thirty years, the Patnaude family has operated one of New Hampshire's southernmost ski areas, **Pat's Peak.** The mountain doesn't have the altitude of the White Mountains ski areas, but it has nineteen trails that are well-groomed and well-divided among the different skill levels. The food in the base lodge is homemade, and it's the kind of family ski area where you don't mind your kids skiing alone. A season pass is good at King Ridge, Mount Sunapee, and Temple Mountain under the "Ski First Mountains New Hampshire" plan. Ski school, nursery, rentals, and other facilities are offered, and ticket sales are limited to the number of people that the lifts can comfortably handle without overcrowding. Write Pat's Peak, Route 114, Henniker 03242 or call (603) 428–3245 or (800) 258–3218.

For lunch in town, stop at Daniel's for innovative sandwiches in their riverside dining room or at **The Bakery** for spinach and cheese croissants, chili, soup, or pizza. Breakfasts are a bargain at $1.00 for coffee and a homemade muffin. A breakfast sandwich of egg with sausage or ham and cheese with coffee is under $2.00. Their lemon poppy seed muffins are delectable. Open Monday through Saturday, 6:00 A.M. to 9:00 P.M., with pizza served after 4:00 p.m only. You'll find it across from the fire department in Henniker (603–428–3120).

Fine dining and lodging are only a bit out of town at the **Colby Hill Inn,** a rambling New England hostelry that has been updated and renovated without losing its country inn flavor. The sixteen guest rooms, each with a private bath, are decorated with antiques. Details of decor and hospitality are all there—elegant bed linens, a full cookie jar, plenty of public rooms, and spontaneous and gregarious hosts. The location is perfect, surrounded by meadows and a backyard where you can watch pheasants as you sit in the perennial garden. In the winter, part of the backyard becomes a skating rink for guests. This is a full service inn, so its prices are higher than those of a typical bed and breakfast, at $85.00 for a double, including a full country breakfast.

The dining room at Colby Hill Inn serves dinner to the public as well as to inn guests—and a fine dinner, too. The salmon is grilled to perfection, the veal marsala tender, and the pork loin flamed in applejack and Amaretto. Service is very personal, but neither stifling nor too folksy—and the view from the dining room of the floodlit barn and carriage shed and clumps of white birches is lovely even in the drab gray of a snowless November evening. Dinner prices are in the upper moderate range, with most entrees $15.00 to $20.00. The dining room is open year-round, Wednesday through Saturday, 5:30 to 8:30 P.M. and Sunday

4:30 to 7:30 P.M. Write Colby Hill Inn, The Oaks, Henniker 03242 or call (603) 428–3281.

The entire Contoocook valley abounds with antique shops, and the Fibre Studio features hand-dyed yarns and supplies for spinning, weaving, and knitting as well as hand-woven fabrics and sheep-related gifts. It's at 9 Foster Hill Road in Henniker (603–428–7830).

The Souhegan Valley

Water power was central to New Hampshire industry from the earliest days, and **Frye's Measure Mill** is still operated by an upright turbine driven by water from two ponds. Actively engaged in the making of fine round and oval wooden boxes, just as the first ones were made here in 1858, the mill also operates Saturday tours in the summer. The mill shop sells the boxes made here as well as other early crafts. Open May 1 to December 15, from 10:00 A.M. to 4:00 P.M. The mill is on Davisville Road and Burton Highway in Wilton; call (603) 654–6581 for more information.

At **Impressions Pottery,** Bob and Amy Oxford create pottery with native wildflowers pressed into the surfaces of the pots. The effect is lovely, with delicate, incised designs and soft colors on a creamy natural background. They make pitchers, clocks, lamps, and a variety of dishes. You can watch them work at their barn studio year-round Thursday through Saturday, 10:00 A.M. to 4:00 P.M. and by appointment, at 123 South Street (Route 13), Milford (603–673–5167).

Off the Beaten Path in the Monadnock Region

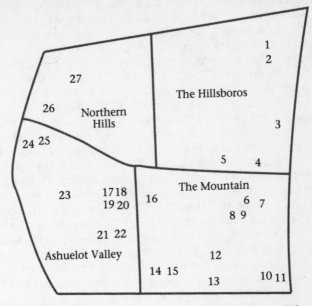

1. Hillsboro Center
2. Fox State Forest
3. Maitre Jacq Restaurant
4. Greenfield State Park
5. The John Hancock Inn
6. Peterborough Historical Society Museum
7. Temple Mountain Ski Area
8. Kernal Bakery
9. Latacarta
10. Barrett House
11. Estelle M. Glavey Antiques
12. Benjamin Prescott Inn
13. Cathedral of the Pines
14. Amos J. Blake House
15. Rhododendron State Park
16. Homestead Bookshop
17. Wyman Tavern
18. Barry Faulkner mural
19. Horatio Colony House Museum
20. Monadnock Children's Museum
21. Covered bridges
22. Swanzey Historical Museum
23. Chesterfield Gorge
24. Park Hill
25. Stuart and John's Sugar House
26. Old Academy Museum
27. Bascom's Sugar House

The Monadnock Region

Word has it that Mount Monadnock is no longer the second most climbed mountain in the world. With motorized access to Fujiyama's summit, fewer people are climbing it, so Monadnock may be number one. Whichever, its rocky ledge summit on a fine summer day is definitely not off the beaten path. But its broad-shouldered cone standing alone with no other mountains for company is the focal point for an entire region. Views of it provide the backdrop for towns miles away, from Jaffrey, where most of the mountain lies, to Keene. On clear days it can be seen from as far away as Boston and the Green Mountains of Vermont.

Geologically, the mountain is the definitive *monadnock,* a mass of rock more durable, hence more resistant to erosion and glacial action, than the land around it. It is this mountain for which the geological phenomenon was named. The rest of the land of this southwest corner of New Hampshire is rolling, accented with small mountains and lakes. Only one city, Keene, is located in the entire area. It, and Peterborough, "Our Town" of Thornton Wilder's play, provide the cultural and business centers, but the smaller towns are surprisingly active, with their own museums, concert series, theater groups, and events. The bandstands that decorate the commons of Monadnock's towns are not there just to take pictures of. Painters, writers, and musicians have found a haven in this area for a century, giving it a rich tradition in the arts.

The Hillsboros

Visitors from outside of New England often comment on the apparent lack of originality displayed in the naming of towns here. In one area will be found town after town with the same name prefixed by the four points of the compass, *Center, Upper,* or *Lower,* or suffixed by *Falls, Mills, Junction, Street,* or *Depot.* The reason has to do with the town system of government often based upon the original land grants. Large parcels of land were settled with several villages springing up within the boundaries of a town. Hillsboro is a good example. Within the limits of the town are Hillsboro, Hillsboro Center, Hillsboro Upper Village, and Hillsboro Lower Village.

Hillsboro Center is among New Hampshire's loveliest towns, its houses set around a circular road on a slight slope, with two churches. The entire center of the village is webbed with stone walls, testament to the number of rocks that northern New Englanders have had to pull out of their farmlands over the centuries. A well-preserved town pound, built to keep stray animals out of neighbors' gardens, completes this almost perfect village scene. Antique shops and a pewter studio are the only signs of commercial activity. Just outside of town, rows of nearly perfect double stone fences border the fields of two exceptionally beautiful hillside farms.

Fox State Forest is a 1,448-acre area of managed forest which contains plantations of exotics (trees that do not grow here naturally) and some unusual protected natural areas as well. One of these is a black gum, or tupelo, swamp. The tree is common to the south but rarely found in New England. A ravine of mature hemlock and one of the state's rare stands of virgin forest are here, as well as a true sphagnum bog formed by a floating mat of moss filled with rare wild plants. More than 20 miles of hiking trails wind through the forest; one of the trails has labels that identify tree species. Cross-country skiers are welcome on the trails in the winter (some of them are quite challenging), but there are no other recreation facilities here, since this is a forest, not a park. You are welcome to picnic on the grounds (they have a few tables) as long as you respect the "carry-in, carry-out" policy. Open year-round from dawn to dusk. Look inside the mailbox by the entrance for a trail guide. Write Fox State Forest, Hillsboro Center Road, P.O. Box 1175, Hillsboro 03244 or call (603) 464–3453 for more information.

The boyhood home of Franklin Pierce, New Hampshire's only native son to become president of the United States, is just off Route 9 at the Lower Village. The mansion is a more elegant one than was common in rural New Hampshire when it was built in 1804. Open Memorial Day to Columbus Day, Saturdays, 10:00 A.M. to 4:00 P.M., Sundays 1:00 to 4:00 P.M., and Fridays in July and August, 10:00 A.M. to 4:00 P.M. It's on Route 31 at Route 9 in Hillsboro (603–478–3165).

The lunch counter at the rear of The Corner Store at the same crossroads serves good blueberry muffins and generous sandwiches. Don't expect a check—just go out to the store cashier and tell her what you had. As you go west on Route 9, look for an outstanding example of a double-stone arch bridge beside the road. It's worth a stop here to walk around to the upstream side for a better picture of what it looked like in the nineteenth century. You can go down under the present bridge to see the stonework of the old bridge as well as the river as it continues downstream through a mass of giant boulders.

It's hard to spot the discreet sign for **Maitre Jacq Restaurant** on Route 47 between Bennington and Francistown, and the building that houses it looks more like a well-kept home. Inside, it is pure French with a menu full of classic dishes with an original touch. A dish of crudités, olives, cornichons, and herbed cheese comes with the menu. The appetizer of steamed mussels in shallots and white wine is enough for a full meal, and the terrine of veal with cognac has just the right texture. Double breast of chicken is roasted with Boursin and crabmeat, or sauteed with mushrooms and cream or Calvados. There will be at least one veal dish, roast duckling, and scallops under a melt-in-the-mouth pastry. The bouillabaisse is solid with shrimps, scallops, clams, and mussels. The entree prices include your choice of appetizer, dessert, and espresso, so there is nothing to do but order a slice of Frangelico cheesecake or a creamy chocolate mousse. The chef-owner is careful about details and fanatical about ingredients. As soon as he can push a trowel into the ground in the spring he begins growing vegetables and herbs for his kitchen. The wine list is well chosen, and the wines, available by the glass or by the bottle, are moderately priced. Considering that the menu prices include three full courses, the $15.00 to $20.00 prices are at the lower end of the moderate range. Open Tuesday through Sunday for dinner only; it's best to make reservations since the restaurant is small and it's far from any second choices. You'll find it at Route 47 and Mountain Road in Francistown; call (603) 588–6655.

Greenfield State Park reserves one sandy beach just for campers who have settled into its spacious, wooded tent sites and has another one for day visitors and picnickers. This is one of the rare places where you can rent a boat either for the fishing or to enjoy the quiet of Otter Lake. One of the smaller of New Hampshire's state parks and one of the least known, it is a perfect retreat for nature lovers, swimmers, and those who seek a place to paddle their canoe in peace. Write the park at P.O. Box 203, Greenfield 03047 or call (603) 547–3497.

The white-spired meeting house in Hancock is said to be the most photographed church in the state, although it is hard to understand how such a statistic is determined. The entire town of Hancock invites photography with its neat rows of fine old buildings along the main street. **The John Hancock Inn** recently celebrated its two hundredth anniversary of welcoming travelers. One of the guest rooms has walls painted by the itinerant muralist Rufus Porter, and antiques and mementos of the inn's long history decorate guest rooms and public areas. Accommodating hosts and a good dining room make this a pleasant inn for a few days of wandering the back roads in the area or browsing in Hancock's Historical Society Museum and antique shops. Rates are moderate in the "inns" category; open all year except for a week in early spring and one after foliage season. Write The John Hancock Inn, Main Street, Hancock 03449 or call (603) 525–3318.

The Mountain

Historical societies perform several valuable services to their towns, such as storing and preserving records of long-closed schools and businesses, providing a safe home for old photographs, maps, and books that would otherwise be lost, and offering a clearinghouse for historical and genealogical information. A few maintain museums based on purchases or gifts of local artifacts, furnishings, and property.

The **Peterborough Historical Society Museum** is one of the finest historical museums of any society in the state. Along with exhibition rooms featuring early tools, Indian artifacts, and antiques, they have in the several buildings of their complex a complete Victorian parlor, a replica of a country store, a colonial-era kitchen, and a restored mill house. Open year-round, Monday through Friday, 1:00 to 4:00 P.M. Tours available June through October. Admission is $1.00; children under twelve are admitted free. The museum is at 19 Grove Street (P.O. Box 58), Peterborough 03458 (603–924–3235).

Temple Mountain Ski Area is small, friendly, and one of the best places for kids to learn to ski. Instructors here seem to have a special knack for getting kids who are barely old enough to stand up on feet to be able to stand up on skis. Lifts are fast, and everybody here smiles. Ski rentals and special beginners' packages are available, and the chili in their slope-side lodge is hearty enough to keep you skiing until the lifts close, which is at 10:00 P.M. Night skiing is especially fun since you can watch the lights twinkle on through the whole valley. Temple Mountain is on Route 101 in Peterborough; call (603) 924–6949.

The Sheiling Forest provides pleasant walking through fields and forests, following stone walls built by long-ago farmers trying to clear their fields of the oversupply of granite boulders that New Hampshire was blessed with. They are easy, level walks. On Saturdays there are programs for small woodlot owners on the care and management of woodlands. Open daily dawn to dusk year-round on Old Street Road in Peterborough.

Peterborough residents evidently have a taste for good food, since there are a number of culinary delights in town. The **Kernal Bakery** was making flaky croissants for Monadnock-region breakfast tables long before *croissant* became a household word. And they are half the price of inferior products elsewhere. Their doughnuts, Danish, cookies, Eccles cakes, and breads are sold out twice a day—they close midday to concentrate on baking more. You can get a cup of coffee here to go with your breakfast pastry, but alas, not a cup of tea. Closed Sunday, Monday, and middays. You'll find the Kernal Bakery on Jaffrey Road (Route 202) in Peterborough; call (603) 924–7930.

The Peterborough Diner on Depot Street is a real shiny silver diner—the kind with wedges of pie in a little glass case on the counter—and it opens at 6:00 A.M. every day of the week (603–924–6202). For quality take-out with an international flair, go to Twelve Pine in a little cottage next to the Unitarian Church on Summer Street. It's open Monday through Friday, 11:00 a.m to 6:00 p.m, and Saturday, 11:00 A.M. to 3:00 P.M. (603–924–6140). The church, by the way, was designed by Bulfinch and is one of New England's finest examples of early New England church architecture. All Saints Episcopal Church on Concord Street, a transitional Gothic building of local granite, is on the National Historic Register.

But back to food. **Latacarta** defies classification. Just as you assume from the gyoza dumplings, the teppanyaki beef, and the tempura that it's Japanese, your eye catches the fettucini and shrimp or the hummus, or the nachitos, enchiladas, Bavarian chicken, or fish and chips. Then the first dish arrives, beautifully presented as a work of art, and you're sure again that it must be Japanese. But the helpings are too generous for that. Whatever the inspiration for each dish, it's cooked to perfection. Salads are a glorious mélange of whole crisp leaves from Rosaly Bass's organic garden up the hill. Seafood tastes as though it had swum into the kitchen. Try to go on a night when Ted Mann is playing classical guitar—he's every bit as good as the food, and the two arts complement each other. Prices are moderate and the menu changes weekly. Open 11:00 a.m to 2:00 P.M. and 5:00 to 9:00 P.M. Tuesday through Sunday. A small adjoining cafe serves light dishes before and after dinner hours. Latacarta is at 6 School Street in Peterborough; call (603) 924–6878.

In New Ipswich, an early textile town on the upper reaches of the Souhegan River, stands one of New England's most extraordinary historic homes. The most outstanding feature of **Barrett House,** or Forest Hall as the Barrett family called it, is that it is not restored, but is completely original, including its furnishings. The house was built about 1800 as a wedding gift, and the story is told that the bride's father agreed to furnish "as large and fine a house" as the groom's father could afford to build. The original furnishings were supplemented by later generations with equally good taste until it was donated by the family to The Society for the Protection of New England Antiquities in 1948. A collection of early musical instruments includes a glass harmonica, invented by Benjamin Franklin. The movie *The Europeans,* based upon the Henry James novel, was filmed here. Open June 1 through October 15, Thursday through Sunday, 12:00 noon to 5:00 P.M. Admission charges are adults, $2.50; seniors, $2.00; and children twelve and under, $1.50. The house is on Main Street in New Ipswich.

In the same town there is another house filled with antiques, but these are all for sale. **Estelle M. Glavey Antiques** fills an entire home, not with showrooms, but with fully furnished rooms of museum-quality antiques. There is no jumble of merchandise. Everything, from the oriental rug on the floor to the china on the table and the flame-stitched wing chair by the fire, is just as it would be in a home—but all for sale and clearly tagged with a price, not a code. The surprise is that the pieces are very reasonably priced, considering their quality and condition. Open all year daily except Monday on Route 124 (603–878–1200).

Windblown Ski Touring Center keeps 20 miles of trails well groomed for cross-country skiers. Along with their waxing shed and restaurant, the center offers a warming hut with "sleeping bag accommodations." The views are spectacular. It's on Route 124, 3 miles west of the town of New Ipswich; call (603) 878–2869 for more information.

West on Route 124, on a slight hill, stands the **Benjamin Prescott Inn.** Instead of buying the collections here, you sleep in them, sit on them, and live among them. The beds may be brass, canopied, or American Empire, and a collection of dolls or fine needlework may decorate the room. Each of the private bathrooms is decorated to match or suit the room it adjoins. A third-floor suite includes a balconied parlor with a Dutch bed as well as a king-sized bed in the adjoining room. The house itself is full of character, with long hallways and corner nooks where you may find some unexpected touch, such as a teddy bear dressed in a bobby's uniform. Full breakfasts include a different entree daily along with home-baked fruit breads. In the kitchen, as in the decorating, little touches delight the senses—in the fall, for example, the French toast is cut in maple-leaf shapes. Each evening guests enjoy handmade candies at bedtime. Prices are moderate to high, beginning at $60.00 for a double, but going as high as $120.00. Write the inn at Route 124 East, Jaffrey 03452 or call (603) 532–6637.

Cathedral of the Pines is an outdoor church as well as a national memorial to those who lost their lives in wartime military service. Services are held here by people of all faiths, using the various altars and wooded "chapels." The Memorial Tower holds a peal of Sheffield bells and a set of four Norman Rockwell bas-reliefs in memory of the women who served in the military services. Even when Cathedral of the Pines is not open for services, you can walk through the grounds, a forest of tall pines atop a hillside, with views of Monadnock, Kearsarge, and southern Vermont. Off Routes 202 and 119 in Rindge; call (603) 899–3300 for more information.

Where other towns may be "postcard towns," Fitzwilliam is a "Christmas card town." Its white town hall and stately homes set around the snow-covered common make it a favorite for artists and photographers creating greeting cards. One of these buildings on the common is the **Amos J. Blake House,** a museum maintained by the Fitzwilliam Historical Society. Built in 1837, this was the home and law office of a well-respected community leader. His law office is intact, and other rooms are furnished in period antiques. A kitchen, parlor, music room, and reconstructed schoolroom are part of the museum, as are displays of military and firefighting memorabilia. A small shop, filled with local crafts, New England food specialties, soaps, and gifts, uses original country store counters, furnishings, and cash register. Admission is free. Open late May to mid-October, Saturday, 10:00 A.M. to 4:00 P.M., and Sunday, 1:00 to 4:00 P.M. Write The Blake House, On the Common (P.O. Box 87), Fitzwilliam 03447 or call (603) 585–3134.

One of the largest stands of wild rhododendrons north of the Allegheny mountains is in Fitzwilliam at **Rhododendron State Park.** The fifteen acres of large shrubs bloom by mid-July in a riot of huge flower clusters against glossy, deep green leaves. At any time of year the trails through this park are bordered by masses of broad evergreen leaves and the thick tangle of trunks and branches that support them. An adjoining wildflower trail was created by the Fitzwilliam Garden Club. Native plants are labeled in the open woodland that borders the path. It is a lovely, quiet, and cool spot, with 1 mile of easy walking. Follow the signs off Route 119. Fitzwilliam has a number of antique shops including a multidealer shop, Strawberry Acres, whose showrooms seem to go on forever. Open 10:00 A.M. to 5:00 P.M., on Route 12 south of town (603–585–6517).

Long on value and view, the Monadnock Mountain View Restaurant in Troy offers a tidy dining room whose chief decor is a full wall of windows overlooking Mount Monadnock. The food is good, with dishes such as chicken Oscar and fish fillets in parchment priced under $10. Open daily for lunch and dinner on Route 12 in Troy (603–242–3300). Gap Mt. Bread, on the Troy common, sells wholegrain breads and serves coffee, tea, and pastries in their small cafe. They also make wonderful granola (603–242–3284).

A back road that branches off Route 12 not far north of the rock ledges gives more views of Monadnock as well as a stone bridge. It brings you to Route 124 and into Marlborough. At the intersection with Route 101 is the **Homestead Bookshop.** This is the secondhand treasury where Harvard students find used books they can't get in Cambridge. Strong in local history, they have several shelves of long-out-of-print books on New Hampshire as well as a travel section well stocked with the works of explorers and adventurers. In addition to nearly 50,000 used books, you will meet the nicest people there. Whatever you're looking for, they'll turn the store upside down to find it. Their book search service ferrets out long-sought books for customers in all parts of the country. Open Monday through Friday, 9:00

A.M. to 5:00 P.M., and Saturday and Sunday, 9:00 A.M. to 4:30 P.M. Call (603) 876–4213 for more information.

Next door in a quonset building is Cheshire Floral Farm, a greenhouse and a good source of unusual dried flowers and wreath-making supplies. In December, stop here for fragrant fresh balsam Christmas trees and wreaths. On Tuesday evenings in the summer there are concerts on the green in front of the library in Marlborough starting at 7:00 P.M. (603–876–4479).

Ashuelot Valley

Keene's main street is lined for several blocks by beautifully cared-for private residences covering all architectural periods since the mid-eighteenth century. In the 1750s, the founders of Keene laid out all of the main lots so that the buildings would be set well back from the center of the highway. That decision set the tone for the development of downtown. At the north end of Main Street stands a large white church with a wedding cake spire. This is one of the most beautiful of New England's churches, and its situation at the head of Central Square gives it a commanding presence.

On the west side of Main Street is the ochre-colored eighteenth-century **Wyman Tavern.** It was from this tavern that a contingent of Keene Minutemen departed to join in the Revolution on April 23, 1775, four days after the battle at Concord, Massachusetts. Prior to that, the first trustees' meeting of Dartmouth College was held here. The tavern is now a museum, furnished in the 1770–1820 period. It is open June 1 to Labor Day, Thursday through Saturday, 11:00 A.M. to 4:00 P.M., and the admission is free. You'll find the Wyman Tavern at 339 Main Street in Keene (603–357–3855).

A short distance up the street from the tavern is Elliot Hall. The large brick building set back from the street is now part of Keene State College. In the spiral staircase of its front hall is a **Barry Faulkner mural,** depicting Central Square in Keene. Keene has several other examples of the work of this noted muralist. The lobby of Fleet Bank beside the church at the head of Central Square is decorated with his *Men of Monadnock* series. Cheshire County Savings Bank, also on the square, has a large single mural of Main Street at the time of the arrival of the first train in Keene in 1848. The Cheshire Medical Center on Court Street displays

Wyman Tavern, Keene

three smaller mural panels moved from another building, and the Keene Public Library has sketches made for his murals located elsewhere.

Across lower Main Street from Elliot Hall is the Archive Center of the Historical Society of Cheshire County, which includes books, maps, manuscripts, art, and photographs for research on early Keene and surrounding towns. Open Tuesdays and Thursdays, 9:00 A.M. to noon and 1:00 to 4:00 P.M. in Rhodes Hall, 246 Main Street, in Keene; call (603) 352–1895.

One of the state's most unusual "old house" museums is in this same neighborhood, next to St. Bernard's Church on Main Street. The **Horatio Colony House Museum** is not a home restored to one particular period, but the home of a twentieth-century heir to a fortune that allowed him to live the life of a nineteenth-century gentleman of leisure. He traveled all over the world, collecting as he went, with a fine eye and highly cultured tastes. The Oriental art he brought back with him is at home in the 1806 Federal mansion amid the fine eighteenth- and nineteenth-century furnishings. Some of his collections are in glass cases in the ell, while other items are displayed as he lived with them. It is a delightful home to tour, and you will leave feeling that you have known this well-read, well-traveled, and generous gentleman who left his estate for others to enjoy. Open mid-May to mid-October, Tuesday through Saturday, 11:00 A.M. to 4:00 P.M., and Saturdays year-round. Admission is free; park behind the church. The address is 199 Main Street in Keene; call (603) 352–0460.

Right across the street is an informal and inexpensive restaurant known for its sandwiches and soups as well as for its outstanding list of hard-to-find beers. Both the address and the name of the restaurant are 176 Main. Don't be surprised if locals refer to this eatery as "P.C.'s"—old names die hard here. Open daily from 11:30 A.M. to 11:00 P.M. (603–357–3100).

Keene's third historic museum is housed in an outstanding example of a Federal home. The Colony House Museum (same family) contains collections of glassware from some of the nation's earliest glassworks and Hampshire pottery produced in Keene from the 1880s to the 1920s. Staffordshire china, early silver, and documents of the Revolutionary war era round out the museum, which is operated by the Historical Society. Open June to Labor Day, Tuesday through Saturday, 11:00 A.M. to 4:00 P.M., and Saturdays only Labor Day to Columbus Day. Admission is

$1.00 for adults; children are admitted free. It's at 104 West Street in Keene (603–357–0889).

You don't have to be a child to enjoy the **Monadnock Children's Museum.** Its upbeat, lively atmosphere and timely, colorful exhibits invite touching, exploring, and getting involved. Exhibits change, but you're sure to find fish, bubbles, musical instruments (ever heard a fanny fiddle?), a design-making pendulum, a light table, mineral exhibits, puppets, and a train set. A full schedule of activities, workshops, field trips, craft lessons, musical events, and interactive programs add to the general air of busyness and excitement. In the front yard are a playhouse and wooden boat that kids just can't stay out of. The world room changes times and places as it explores cultures such as Tibet, medieval France and the French heritage, or the Abenaki. Open 10:00 A.M. to 4:00 P.M. every day except holidays; admission is $2.50 no matter how old or young you are. It's a good investment for adults—you'll feel years younger when you leave. The museum is at 147 Washington Street in Keene (603–357–5161).

For lunch in an old-fashioned diner with old-fashioned prices and friendly atmosphere, don't miss Lindy's. Everybody eats here, especially on Fridays when they make fishcakes, right off Main Street on Gilbo Avenue. Open every day 6:00 A.M. to 9:00 P.M. (603–352–4273).

The Fine Arts Center at Keene State College has an active performance schedule (603–357–4041) and Keene supports its own choral group, the Keene Chorale. Their professional-quality concerts are held in the spring and before Christmas and may include sacred works such as masses and oratorios or operatic choral selections. For a schedule of concerts call (603) 357–1534. During the summer, concerts featuring popular bands are held on Wednesday evenings at the bandstand in the common on Central Square from 7:00 to 8:30 P.M. (603–357–9829).

Swanzey, directly south of Keene, has maintained and preserved four **covered bridges** over the Ashuelot River. The following route will show you all of them. Leave Keene on Route 10 (Winchester Street) and turn left on Matthews Road just past the veterinary clinic. Go left at the end and through the first of the bridges. When that road ends, go left again and shortly join Route 32 at the Potash Bowl (remember where this is—we'll get back to it later). All this sounds complicated, but it's only a distance of 3 to 4 miles. Go south on Route 32 to Carleton Road, where you will find

Carlton Bridge, Swanzey Center

another bridge in a few hundred yards. If it's early spring and the water is high, the bridge will be closed, but you can drive down to watch the river lapping at its floorboards. Return to Route 32 and continue south to Swanzey Lake Road on your right. Follow this winding road until it ends at a T. Go left, then right, and you'll pass through the Westport bridge and end up on Route 10 again. Go right until you see the sign for West Swanzey to your right. The fourth bridge is to your left as the street ends at the mill. Back on Route 10, a right will take you back to Keene.

Covered bridges did not originate in New England—they were a common sight in the Alpine regions of Europe for the same reasons early New Englanders built them. The roof protected floorboards and support timbers from the harsh weather and snow buildup which would weaken or break the bridge under its weight. Snow falling on the sloping roof would slide off, as it does on a house roof. The biggest job for road agents was shoveling snow *onto* the bridge so that sleigh runners could slide over them in the time of year when the sleighs replaced carriages and wagons for transport. (In New England, the term "road agent" means the person whose job it is to maintain roads. It does not refer to a highwayman, as it does in many other places.)

Along Route 10, between the Westport bridge and West Swanzey is the **Swanzey Historical Museum,** a newly opened building with some unusually interesting exhibits. Here you will find an operational Amoskeag steam fire pumper made in Manchester and a stagecoach. The museum is wheelchair accessible and is open June through October, Monday to Friday, 1:00 to 5:00 P.M., and Saturdays and Sundays, 10:00 A.M. to 6:00 P.M. on Route 12 in Swanzey; call (603) 352–4579 for more information.

For over fifty years, the town of Swanzey has performed Denman Thompson's *The Old Homestead* at an open-air natural arena known as the Potash Bowl. Thompson's down-home plays, filled with moral lessons and country values, delighted New York theater audiences of the Victorian era. This play, performed each July, is a real period piece. Bring lawn chairs or blankets to sit on. Admission is $5.00 (603–352–0697)

Chesterfield Gorge shows the power of persistence. A relatively small brook has worn a deep gorge through the rocks here as it cascades from pool to pool for a distance of about ¼ mile. It is an easy hike, just over ½ mile, through a forest of beech, birch, and hemlock. A small pavilion at the head of the trail contains information on the geologic history of the gorge's formation. A shady grove provides a good place for a picnic. The gorge is on Route 9, west of Keene.

Farther west, Route 63 crosses, leading south to Chesterfield and the entrance to Pisgah (pronounced "Piz-gee") State Park. The road to this wilderness preserve winds along the edge of a hill through mixed hardwood forests. There are no facilities in the 13,000 acres of this park, and camping is not allowed. Hiking and ski trails criss-cross the area, which is a favorite with fishermen and hunters. For perfectly groomed cross-country ski trails (snow permitting, of course), follow signs to Road's End Farm on Jackson Hill Road. Its beautiful location on top of a hill gives you views over Pisgah Park, Mount Monadnock, and to Mount Snow in Vermont. Rental equipment is available, and the farm kitchen offers soups, sand-wiches, and hot drinks. Everyone enjoys the easygoing, gregarious hosts, who will gladly show how it's done if you've never skied before. Open weekends and holidays 9:00 A.M. to 5:00 P.M.; call (603) 363–4703 for snow conditions. The trails are available in spring and summer for hiking, and the views are just as good then.

If you follow it northward, Route 63 winds along the shore of Spofford Lake and into Westmoreland (pronounced with the accent on "west") and on through the settlement of **Park Hill,** a cluster of noteworthy early buildings, the likes of which are rare outside of Portsmouth or Exeter. The Meeting House is one of the state's earliest, built in 1762 with a facade and spire considered among the finest in their period of architectural design and detail. The Paul Revere bell was placed there in 1827. Around the church are several early homes, dating from as early as 1774.

Route 63 winds past some of New Hampshire's finest and most fertile farmland, with meadows full of grazing cattle and views across the Connecticut River valley into Vermont. From mid-February until mid-April and from mid-September until the end of November you can stop for breakfast, lunch, or a snack at **Stuart and John's Sugar House.** It's best in late February and into March when the sap is running and the back room is filled with steam from the evaporators. The corn fritters and homemade doughnuts are delicious, and syrup comes in a full-sized milk pitcher that the waitress plunks on the table when she brings the menu. All you need to decide is what to pour it over. If it's not breakfast or lunch time when you are passing by, try a maple sun-dae, frappe, or, in the fall, maple apple pie. This place isn't fancy;

you sit on folding chairs at church supper-style tables. It's family style, family run, and a favorite low-cost Sunday outing for local families. Open weekends only, until 3:00 P.M. on Route 63 at Route 12 in Westmoreland (603–399–4486).

Northern Hills

Walpole looks down onto Route 12, and this picture-perfect village is a good place to stroll through and admire the beautifully preserved and maintained eighteenth- and nineteenth-century homes that encircle the green. On Sunday evenings during July and August, band concerts fill this grassy common with music and people.

The prosperity that built the many homes and public buildings in Walpole resulted from the building of a canal around the Great Falls of the Connecticut River in 1790, which allowed river traffic (water was the main means of moving goods in those days) to proceed past here to the north country. The heirlooms of many of these early families have found their way to the **Old Academy Museum.** Silk dresses with the kind of needlework that only prosperous women had the time to pursue have been preserved here along with furniture, tools, utensils, and kitchenware and a completely restored schoolroom from the original academy. Canton china, Shaker furniture, and the original piano mentioned in *Little Women,* a gift to the Alcott sisters when they were living in Walpole, are just a few of the treasures that have been presented to the museum. A small shop carries one-of-a-kind crafts, such as traditional hickory-nut dolls dressed in period costumes. Open from 2:00 to 4:00 P.M. Saturday and Sunday in July and August on Main Street in Walpole; call (603) 756–3449 for more information.

For a peek inside one of those beautiful homes around the green, stay at the 1801 House, a bed and breakfast with private baths and good old-fashioned Yankee breakfasts on non-school days. Weekdays during the school year, a continental breakfast is served. Everyone loves their collie dog and the big Concord woodstove in the kitchen. Rates are low, especially at a location like Walpole, starting at $30.00 per night. The 1801 House is on Washington Square; call (603) 756–9055.

On Saturdays, stop at the Bellows House Bakery for cookies (nine varieties), French breads, muffins, and brownies. It is open from

8:00 a.m to 2:00 P.M. Saturdays only, on North Main Street at High Street, Walpole (603–756–4250).

If you have a spare day and a sense of adventure, you could take any road out of Walpole and follow it until it ends in the dooryard of a farmhouse or bumps into Route 12A. The hillsides are covered with well-kept farms and are separated by lovely little hollows. The views over the valley are beautiful when you reach the hillcrests, most of which have been cleared for pasture land. North of Walpole, Route 123 heads into more hills, following the Cold River (*all* rivers here are cold; one wonders who decided that this one should be so honestly named). From the village of Drewsville, a road heads north toward Langdon, and in about a mile it passes New Hampshire's shortest covered bridge, only 36 feet long.

East of Alstead on Route 123A is another covered bridge and signs for **Bascom's Sugar House.** From mid-March through the first week in April, while the sap runs, Bascom's evaporators, both the ultramodern osmo-separators and the old-fashioned steaming pans, produce syrup that will be shipped all over the world. It's a warm steamy place to be on a windy March day, and after you've watched sap becoming syrup, you can sample the traditional New England treat, sugar on snow. Actually, it's syrup on snow, and it makes a chewy candy that is always served with a dill pickle to balance its sweetness. Doughboys with syrup, maple pecan pie, and maple milkshakes are available here, and you can eat them at long tables covered with red-checked oilcloth. Bascom's sells syrup, maple cream, and candies throughout the year and will ship gifts for you as well. At any time of year it's well worth the trip to this beautiful hilltop setting just for the view. For an even better panorama, walk five minutes to the top of the pasture, where there is a 50-mile view across the meadow and maple groves into Vermont. Maple treats served March and early April (call to make sure the run has begun), Saturday and Sunday, 11:00 A.M. to 5:00 P.M. Write Bascom's at R.R. 1, Box 138, Alstead 03602 or call (603) 835–2230 or 835–6361. Syrup and candy are sold during regular business hours on weekdays year-round.

Off the Beaten Path in the Dartmouth-Sunapee Region

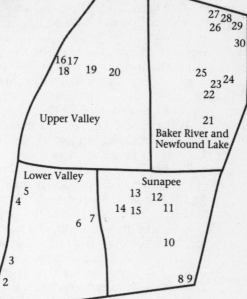

1. The Fort at No. 4
2. Morningside Flight Park
3. West Claremont
4. Northstar Canoe Livery
5. Studio of Augustus St. Gaudens
6. The Library Arts Center
7. Dorr Mill Store
8. Fall Foliage Festival
9. Mt. Kearsarge Indian Museum
10. Nunsuch Dairy
11. Andover Historical Museum
12. The English House
13. La Meridiana
14. Cricenti's Bog
15. New London Inn
16. Baker Memorial Library
17. Hood Museum of Art
18. The Hanover Inn
19. Lower Shaker Village
20. Canaan Street
21. Profile Falls
22. Wellington State Park
23. Hebron Marsh Wildlife Sanctuary
24. Paradise Point Nature Center
25. Sculptured Rocks
26. The Quincy Bog
27. Town Pound
28. Mr. Jacquith's Garden
29. Crabapple Inn

The Dartmouth-Sunapee Region

The Connecticut River flows through a broad flat valley as it forms the border between New Hampshire and neighboring Vermont. Along its shores and up the hillsides that overlook it are sprawling farmlands: fields of corn, herds of cattle, truck farms, and family farms. Their massive barns and tall, round silos punctuate the landscape. These venerable homes were built by some of the earliest settlers in the valley.

The farms were not always so serene. The river was the major artery of travel for the Indians as well as the settlers, and the French and Indian War was fought along its banks. The stockade fence of The Fort at No. 4, in Charlestown, is a reminder of those days. It was to educate Indians that Eleazer Wheelock founded a school that now is Dartmouth College. The influence of that college and of Colby-Sawyer College in nearby New London on the entire upper valley area is significant, especially in the performing and fine arts they attract.

To the east of the Connecticut River valley rise the gentle slopes of Mounts Sunapee, Kearsarge, Cardigan—all about 3,000 feet in altitude—and other smaller mountains. The Appalachian Trail crosses the Connecticut on its way south, and nearly every mountain in the region, however small, has a trail to its summit.

Lakes dot the landscape. The largest of them is Sunapee, which, despite its position as a major summer playground, has never taken on a "Coney Island" atmosphere. Its shores are still clad in trees; cottages rather than resorts house most of its summer visitors. This region is a quiet part of the state, and even the interstate that bisects it hasn't changed that. In fact, from the time that I-89 leaves Concord until it arrives in Lebanon, at the Vermont border, there is almost no commercial activity visible along its sides, only miles of forest and farmland backed by mountain vistas.

The Lower Valley

The Fort at No. 4 was once the northernmost English-speaking village in the New World. The museum today is an authentic reconstruction of the settlement founded there in 1746. It is New England's only living history museum of the period of the French and Indian War. Within its log stockade are furnished province houses and shops where costumed interpreters carry on the daily work of an isolated colonial village. Dinner is prepared in a huge open fireplace, candles are dipped, and wool and flax spun and woven. From the lookout tower sentries kept watch over the river and valley for signs of attack by the Indians or the French. The skirmishes that took place here in those early years are recreated in full costume each year, and a cloud of smoke from musket fire hangs over the river as it did two and one-half centuries ago when, in 1747, it was besieged by a force of four hundred, but withstood the attack. This success resulted in the withdrawal of French forces to Canada and the beginning of English supremacy in northern New England. Of particular interest here are the herb garden and the blacksmith shop, where a master smith creates the tools and utensils necessary for daily life and work on the frontier. A museum shop carries items of the period at extraordinarily reasonable prices. Look here for pottery, blown glass, museum reprints, books on colonial life and skills, and kits for learning early crafts. Open daily from Mother's Day through foliage season in October, from 10:00 A.M. to 5:00 P.M. every day except Tuesday. Admission is $6.00 for adults and $4.00 for children ages six to eleven. The Fort at No. 4 is on Route 11 (Box 336), Charlestown 03603; call (603) 826–5700.

Charlestown's main street is lined with distinguished old homes, many of which date from the early 1800s. The Unitarian Church and two of those houses are the work of Stephen Hassam, great-grandfather of the Impressionist painter Childe Hassam, who often painted the Isle of Shoals.

For a well-prepared and inexpensive lunch or dinner, stop at Panhandlers in the middle of town. Their "small" grinders are 10-inch rolls so stuffed with filling that it's hard to hold them together. Even the crabmeat grinder is under $3.00. Check for the daily specials, which may be a homely favorite such as fried tripe or fish filets fresh from the coast. This isn't the elegant restaurant that you'd choose for your birthday dinner, but you won't find nicer people or better food for the price. Open from 11:00 A.M., serving lunch until 3:00 P.M., dinner until 8:00 P.M. Closed Monday. Panhandlers is on Main Street in Charlestown.

North of Charlestown, you can see to the east the steep hillside of **Morningside Flight Park.** If you've always longed to test the air currents on your own set of wings, they offer instruction on hang-gliding at their 450-foot flying site. Visitors are welcome to watch the steady procession of takeoffs and landings. Morningside is on Route 12 in Charlestown; call (603) 542–4416 for further details.

Claremont's early settlers quickly saw the potential of the water-falls in the Sugar River as it flows from Lake Sunapee to the Connecticut River. The first dam was built in 1767 for a grist and saw mill, and other plants soon followed, their machinery powered by the force from the 300-foot drop in the river as it passes through town. Mill buildings still dominate the center of Claremont.

To the west, about 3 miles on Route 103, is the settlement of **West Claremont.** A road to the left leads across an old dam with mill foundations and again left to two historic churches. Union Church, a large, white clapboard building with curved windows, is the oldest Episcopal church building in New Hampshire. Considering that the Church of England was the established church during this period, one wonders why St. John's in Portsmouth doesn't have this distinction. The answer is that the original St. John's burned and was rebuilt. It is still a surprise to see the oldest one this far inland—and this far from any present-day settlement. Its only neighbor, directly across the street, is St. Mary's Church, the first Roman Catholic church in the state, built between 1823 and 1825. The priest who established St. Mary's parish was the son of the Episcopal rector of Union Church across the street. The son had converted to Catholicism. The two men conducted a school for the children of West Claremont mill workers in the second floor of St. Mary's.

Today, these vanguard churches stand alone, surrounded only by West Part Burying Ground, the settlement they once served long gone.

The Connecticut River flows peacefully between its wooded shores, perfect for traveling by canoe. You can rent a canoe at **Northstar Canoe Livery** in Cornish for half-day, full-day, or overnight trips on the Connecticut. The livery provides a shuttle that carries canoes and passengers upstream to put-ins either 4 or 12 miles distant. The 12-mile trip takes four to four and one-half hours; canoe rental and the shuttle are $17.00 per person. An overnight trip can be arranged so that you can camp on an island in the middle of the river. (You're still in New Hampshire, since New Hampshire owns to the normal high-water mark on the Vermont side. When it floods, Vermont owns the excess.) Northstar Canoe Livery is at Balloch's Crossing, Route 12A, in Cornish (603–542–5802).

The bridge across the Connecticut at Cornish is the longest covered bridge in the United States. (The longest in New Hampshire is at Bath; this one doesn't count since its other end is in Vermont.) Built in 1886, it traverses the river in two spans and has an unusual timber lattice truss construction. At the turn of this century, Cornish was the home of a thriving colony of artists, writers, poets, and patrons who built or purchased summer homes around the **studio of Augustus St. Gaudens.** Italian terraced gardens surrounded old farmhouses, and the summer season's social life was one of wealthy Bohemia.

The artists are gone, but the genius of the sculptor who attracted them to this retreat lives on in his beautifully situated home, gardens, and studio. His sculptures are displayed throughout the grounds, and even if these don't interest you, this memorial is worth visiting for its gardens and walkways lined with birches and hemlock hedges. Open from 8:30 a.m to 4:30 P.M. every day from Memorial Day through October 31. The grounds remain open until dusk. Admission is $1.00. Write St. Gaudens Memorial, RR #2, Box 73, Cornish 03745 or call (603) 675–2175.

Interest in the arts is strong in this area. In Newport, **The Library Arts Center** has a continuing series of exhibits including fine arts, crafts, and historical works displayed in two galleries. The center offers a regular program of classes and performances as well. Open Tuesday to Saturday, 11:00 A.M. to 4:00 P.M. all year except in January. It's located behind the library at the common, 58 North Main Street in Newport; call (603) 863–3040 for more information.

The **Dorr Mill Store** is well known to rug makers for its remnants of woolens used for hooking and braiding. Along with the fine woolens woven at the mill and sold here at bargain prices, the store carries men's and women's sportswear and quilt-making supplies. On Routes 11 and 103 east of Newport, the shop is open Monday through Saturday, 9:00 A.M. to 5:00 P.M. For more information, write the store at P.O. Box 88, Guild 03754 or call (603) 863–1197.

Sunapee

We have no intention of entering the historical dispute over the original meaning of *sunapee* in the Indian languages. It's a lovely region, in any language, with the mountain and lakes of the same name and the succession of smaller lakes between Mount Sunapee and Mount Kearsarge. To the south lies Warner, with a farmers' market on the Town Hall lawn every Saturday morning from late June through October.

The market culminates in the two-day **Fall Foliage Festival** on Columbus Day weekend, when craftspeople join in and the farmers fill an entire tent with their most tempting harvests. Where else can you find fresh shiitake mushrooms at a farmers' market? A woodsmen's contest and a Sunday parade highlight this annual event, along with chicken and lobster lunches both days.

Some museums are simply collections displayed to share or teach. Others breathe a spirit into those who stop to look. The **Mt. Kearsarge Indian Museum** is one of the latter. Its spirit is probably best summed up in the words of Chief Seattle in the late 1800s: "Every part of the earth is sacred to my people. . . every shining pine needle, every sandy shore, every light mist in the dark forest. . . we are part of the earth and it is part of us." The purpose of the museum is not so much to show the artifacts as to interpret the lifestyle through the art and culture and to renew in all of us the positive relationship the Indians knew between the earth and its people. It succeeds. The exhibits are the lifetime collection of Charles (Bud) and Nancy Thompson, who didn't want to have "a mausoleum of pickled artifacts," but rather a museum with a voice.

The voice is that of Indians, and it rings as true today as when the words were spoken. Their feelings about the natural world and our place in it introduce each room in this beautifully housed and displayed collection. Except for the quotations, there are no written labels or signs. Instead, a docent accompanies each visitor or group, explaining the displays focusing on those things that catch the visitors' interest. The emphasis is on the relationship between the Indian and the plants and animals of his environment, and something in this museum is bound to strike a chord with every visitor. The artifacts themselves are incomparable—quillwork, moose hair embroidery, intricate beadwork, wood and bone carving, basketry, canoes, and snow shoes—but the way of life that spawned the art is the real message. A museum shop sells authentic Indian handwork such as rugs, beadwork, and pottery, as well as books for adults and children concerning the various North American Indian tribes. Outdoors, a self-guided walk leads through two acres of native plants and trees used for medicine and food. Open from the first Saturday in May to the Saturday after Thanksgiving, Monday through Saturday, 10:00 A.M. to 5:00 P.M. and Sunday 1:00 to 5:00 P.M. Admission is $5.00 for adults and $3.00 for children ages six to twelve. Write Mt. Kearsarge Indian Museum, Kearsarge Mountain Road, P.O. Box 142, Warner 03278 (603–456–2600).

As you drive New Hampshire's roads you will see a number of domesticated animals from the expected cow to the exotic llama. **Nunsuch Dairy** in South Sutton raises Tagenburg goats. A small dairy by commercial standards, Nunsuch produces rondelles of goat cheese that are sought by the area's top restaurants. You can stop to visit this meticulously clean dairy, meet the enthusiastic owner, Courtney Haase, and let the children go for a ride around the farm in the wooden cart pulled by a goat named Peter. Prices on the cheese are phenomenally low—an eight-ounce rondelle for $2.75 and $6.50 per pound for hard cheese. Pack a chunk of Nunsuch cheese for a lunch when you climb Mount Kearsarge, or take it on a picnic to some shady roadside spot. Nunsuch Dairy is on Route 114, South Sutton 03221; call (603) 927–4176. (Courtney also sells by mail: Nunsuch Dairy, Star Route, Bradford 03221.)

In the Victorian-era railroad station at the village of Potter Place, the **Andover Historical Society Museum** has interesting collections, including an original Western Union Telegraph office. The building itself is intact, a fine example of the ornamented stations that once lined the tracks throughout New England. One of the highlights of the museum is a dugout canoe that is in very good condition; outside on the tracks are a caboose and a plow car used to clear the tracks during snow storms. Open Saturday 10:00 a.m to 3:00 P.M. and Sunday 1:00 to 3:00 P.M.

The English House bed and breakfast in Andover is a little bit of Victorian Surrey transplanted. Its seven guest rooms, two of which are exceptionally large, have private baths, and two share a dormer sitting room with a window seat. This is only one example of the delightful architectural features of this meticulously restored turn-of-the-century home. Its British owners serve a classic full-course English breakfast with an international touch to the dishes, such as a Lebanese fruit compote. They make all of their own breads, fruit preserves, yogurt, and even their own sausage. If you are fond of such English breakfast specialties as oysters, be sure to ask. Gillian loves to share her considerable cooking talents with appreciative guests. Be sure to arrive in time for tea in the parlor.

Along with cooking and welcoming guests, Gillian Smith offers classes and three-day midweek seminars in quilting, dress design, and other techniques in her needlework studio. Cross-country enthusiasts can ski out of the back yard onto a series of well-groomed trails maintained by neighboring Procter Academy. Rental skis are available only 200 yards away in the village. Three downhill ski areas are within a twenty-minute drive.

Ask for the Smiths' map of local antique shops—five of the shops specialize in old books and one in old maps. In fact, The English House maintains a miniature travel office in the guests' lounge, with scrapbooks full of ideas for the guests' entertainment. Write The English House, P.O. Box 162, Andover 03216 or call (603) 735–5987.

La Meridiana in Wilmot is a family-owned restaurant dedicated to the foods of the chef's home in northern Italy. Specialties include a salad of tender calamari in a delicate olive oil dressing, gnocchi in a sauce so good that you'll be tempted to mop up the excess with the crusty Italian bread, and tender white veal with lemon served with lightly poached finocchi. The choice of desserts is equally varied and tempting: chocolate truffles, Italian cheesecake, raspberry-chocolate cheesecake, zuppa inglese, cannoli, or a traditional chocolate sponge cake with ricotta filling. Prices on all courses are inexpensive to moderate, with two-thirds of the entrees under $10.00. The wine list is quite reasonably priced as well. An especially endearing feature is that they suggest sharing a pasta course, so those without a gargantuan appetite can split a dish of risotto, gnocchi, or agnolotti as a first course and still have room for the entree to follow. La Meridiana is on Route 11 and Old Winslow Road in Wilmot; call (603) 526–2033.

In Elkins (take the road marked BUSINESS LOOP), look for Mesa, where you can find bargains on imported pottery and dinnerware at the importer's only outlet store. They have their "yard sales" on some Saturdays; for dates call (603) 526–2127.

New London is the home of Colby-Sawyer College, whose stately campus dominates the southern end of the town's main street. Throughout the school year theater and musical performances keep the local arts scene lively, and then a summer theater takes over the job with Broadway musicals. The town is a good center for hiking and cross-country skiing, with nearly 50 kilometers of trails groomed and managed by Norsk Cross Country. When the ground is not snow-covered, hikers and walkers can choose from among eight or nine trails, leading to or past such varied attractions as a cave, a quarry, cascades, a beaver pond, abandoned farms, and lovely mountain views.

Cricenti's Bog, a pond grown in with sphagnum moss, is located just out of the center of town. It is a fascinating nature reserve where you can observe the unique bog flora from wooden walkways, designed to protect both the fragile flora and your shoes. (It's hard to see the trail sign from the road; it's just opposite the 50 MPH sign after you pass Cricenti's Market.) The town's Nature Park, nearby, has a resident naturalist on duty and a regular schedule of environmental activities for children.

Hiking shoes and ski boots are a common sight at the **New London Inn,** which has been welcoming guests since it opened in 1810 as Sargent's Hotel. Today it is not only a gathering place for guests fresh from the trails, but also a haven for gastronomes. The chef is co-innkeeper, so there is never a "chef's night off" or a "between chefs" to dim the consistent quality of the food. Local vegetables, often grown to the chef's specifications by a neighboring organic farm, free-range pheasants from a Vermont farm, and Nunsuch goat cheese are only a few of the ingredients that Jeff Follansbee has found nearby and uses regularly in ways that continue to delight diners there. Dinner may begin with an appetizer of avocado with jicama and smoked chorizo in a lime and mint sauce, a chilled soup of parsnips with salmon caviar, a duck pâté, or a full-bodied tomato soup, tangy with lemongrass. The pork scallopini melts in the mouth; it is accompanied by a light sauce of sun-dried tomatoes and a crisp pasta fritter. A hot salad of wilted kale with vinaigrette and goat cheese is the perfect foil for grilled spring lamb.

The wine list is excellent, with Alsatian, Australian, and other selections supplementing the expected choices. Thirteen of these are available by the glass—replacing the usual jug wines of most lists—especially nice for a couple wishing to match dinner selections to wines without having to buy several bottles. Prices are moderate, both on the wine list and on the menu. The dining room serves lunch and dinner daily during the summer and fall and daily except Sunday and Monday at other times of the year.

Upstairs, rooms are individually decorated, each with at least one antique piece. Updating has added modern amenities without sacrificing the grace and charm that are the hallmarks of an old inn. A full breakfast is included in the room rates, which are in the moderate range. Children are welcome guests at the inn, which is located on Main Street in New London. Call (603) 526–2791 or (800) 526–2791.

Each June the New London Inn joins with historical societies and inns of the region in the Annual Turn of the Century Weekend. Period costumes, antique cars, ice cream socials, croquet on the lawn, tea with scones, and events at four historical society museums recreate a Sunday afternoon in 1908. Tickets are $5.00 and are available at the inn.

Upper Valley

The town of Hanover and Dartmouth College are clustered around a large green, decorated in winter by a giant ice sculpture if the weather cooperates. Overlooking this from a slight hill are the white buildings of the original college. Two of the remaining sides are lined with red brick college buildings, among them Baker library. The south side is divided between the Hanover Inn and the Hopkins Center for the Performing Arts. In and around that quadrangle lies an amazing wealth of art.

In the basement of **Baker Memorial Library** is a series of frescoes completed in 1934 by the Mexican artist Jose Clemente Orozco. A free brochure describing the frescoes is available at the central desk. They are powerful, and since their recent cleaning and restoration, true to their original brilliant colors. They were quite controversial in the 1930s but are now appreciated as a rare art treasure. Even less well known than the frescoes is the Hickmott Shakespeare Collection, also housed at Baker Library. This is in the special collections room, open 8:00 A.M. to 4:30 P.M. Monday through Friday. The gift of Allerton C. Hickmott, the collection includes all four of the folio editions, close to forty quarto editions, all of the pre-1700 editions of *Macbeth,* and many other early editions. Also in the library's treasure room is Daniel Webster's set of John James Audubon's *Birds of America* in a folio first edition, over 150 titles of incunabula (works printed before 1501), a 1439 Bible, and a collection of over 200 volumes illustrating the art of fine book binding. These include embossed leather, gold embroidery, miniatures, and volumes with painted fore edges.

Adjoining the Hopkins Center is the new **Hood Museum of Art**. For many years, Dartmouth was unable to exhibit even its most priceless art treasures because it lacked a building for them. Now built, this museum contains galleries for collections of American, European, African, Indian, and ancient art. The collection of Assyrian reliefs from the ninth century B.C. is outstanding, rivaled in New England by only one other series. At the other end of history, the Hood is one of the very few American museums to own the entire suite of Picasso's Vollard etchings. There are Roman mosaics, paintings of the Italian Renaissance, baroque period, Hudson River school, and representative pieces from every major style and period. There is almost always a traveling exhibit, as well, often incorporating pieces from Dartmouth's own collections.

In 1991 the museum acquired the most comprehensive private collection of Melanesian art in the country. Nearly one thousand objects from Papua New Guinea and Vanuatu, ranging in size from miniatures to monumental sculptured works over 8 feet tall and 14-foot drums, the collection is both comprehensive and rich in detail. Open all year, Tuesday through Friday, 11:00 A.M. through 5:00 P.M., Saturday and Sunday 9:30 to 5:00 P.M. Write The Hood Museum, Hanover 03755 or call (603) 646–2808.

The Hopkins Center next door is as broad in its performing arts offerings as the Hood is in the fine arts. The schedule includes choral and symphonic music, ballet, opera, jazz, chamber music, and puppeteers.

The Hanover Inn is an institution almost as revered as the college itself. Whenever the inn changes so much as a carpet, some old grad notices and comments. That has not stopped the inn from undertaking renovations to keep it up to date with modern amenities such as phones with modem ports. As the oldest continuously operated business in New Hampshire, the inn treads a careful balance between maintaining its historical flavor and providing luxurious accommodations and service that anticipates every need. Rooms are elegant, some with real marble baths and such details as clothing stands and low wattage lights. The Daniel Webster room serves highly recommended meals at well-spaced tables in a carpeted pink and gray Edwardian setting.

If you are a celebrity watcher, you can get the autograph of anyone performing or speaking at the Hopkins Center by waiting in the corridor that connects it with the inn. They all stay at the inn and use this private lower-level passageway before and after appearances.

Expect to pay well for rooms in this top-rated hotel, but expect also to get your money's worth. Special packages include free passes at the Dartmouth skiway and other bonuses, so be sure to ask. Write The Hanover Inn, On the Green, Hanover 03755; call (603) 643–4300 or (800) 443–7024.

Hanover is considered one of the best towns for shopping, its Main Street lined with independent, locally owned shops. It's a wonderful place to browse year-round, and you can never tell what you will find in the next store. Eating places abound, most of them quite good. At Cafe la Fraise, the flair is generally French, but you will find homemade pasta and perhaps a Thai or other exotic dish. It is one of the few restaurants open on Monday evenings, an important fact for any traveler to know. You'll find it at 8 West Wheelock Street in Hanover; call (603) 643–8588.

The **Lower Shaker Village** at Enfield, while not as extensive as the one at Canterbury, is of special interest for its stone architecture. The largest Shaker dwelling house in existence, four and one-half stories tall, is now the Shaker Inn, which has a restaurant downstairs and inexpensive guest accommodations in the austere upper floors. These rooms have the sparse simplicity and built-in cabinets that are hallmarks of Shaker design. Write The Shaker Inn, Enfield 03748 or call (603) 632–5466.

The museum portion is best known for its herb gardens and for the regular series of workshops in Shaker arts, industries, and gardening held there throughout the year. In early June, a Festival of Shaker Crafts and Herbs features plants, herbal and Shaker crafts, demonstrations, and programs on herb gardening and cooking, with herb growers from all parts of New Hampshire and Vermont. Open June 1 to October 15, Monday through Saturday, 10:00 A.M. to 5:00 P.M., Sunday 12:00 to 5:00 P.M., and weekends only through the winter. Admission is $3.50 for adults, $2.50 for seniors, and $1.50 for young people aged ten to eighteen. It's on Route 4A in Enfield; call (603) 632–4346 for more information.

Northwest from the village of Canaan is the unusual settlement of **Canaan Street.** The main, and only, street is lined on both sides with a mile of distinguished white homes and churches. These date from as early as 1794. Behind the single row of homes on the east is a lake, and in the other direction is a sweeping view over the valley to the Green Mountains of Vermont. Wide lawns surround the homes, and the broad street is lined with maples and stone walls. The entire scene, so unexpectedly encountered, seems to have been dropped there from the last century.

Baker River and Newfound Lake

New Hampshire is filled with stone profiles, and although none rivals the fame of the Old Man of the Mountains in Franconia Notch, each has its degree of local renown. Some require a great deal of imagination or at least a view from the right spot to distinguish. **Profile Falls,** 2½ miles south of Bristol on Route 3A, is one of these, but even without spotting the profile, the falls themselves are well worth the short walk. Turn off Route 3A to the east (left if you're traveling south) just before the bridge with the small sign for the falls. A short distance down the road is another small sign and a pull-out area, but it is steep and slippery, and we suggest parking along the road just before the sign; there is space for cars to pull over just after you turn off the main road. You can either follow the road to the trail or follow the snowmobile trail, which also leads to the base of the falls. The drop is about 40 feet over a broad ledge, and the profile is supposed to be at the foot of the falls in silhouette against the white water. On hot days, local boys can often be found jumping from the high rocks on the right into the pool at the base of the falls. We don't recommend that you try it.

North of Bristol on Route 3A is a picnic area maintained by the Rotary Club, in a grove of pines. Shortly past this a road leads to West Shore Road, which hugs the shore of Newfound Lake and offers lovely views of the lake and mountains. Along the road, on a point of land surrounded by the unusually clear waters of the lake, is one of New Hampshire's finest and perhaps least known beaches. **Wellington State Park** has a fine sandy beach under tall pines, so you can choose sun or shade and still be at the water's edge. Along with picnic tables, there is a snack bar. You can't launch boats from the park, but you can put in canoes or small sailing craft easily. It is a busy, friendly park with plenty of beach and water, so it never seems crowded. It's open 9:00 A.M. to 8:00 P.M. on weekends from Memorial Day to the last week of June and for the two weeks after Labor Day. During the rest of the summer it's open every day at the same hours.

At the northern end of the lake, between the attractive village of Hebron and Route 3A, is the **Hebron Marsh Wildlife Sanctuary.** You can park down the dirt road just before the red cottage while you visit the diverse wildlife habitats of freshwater marsh, open fields, and the banks of the Cockermouth River. Follow signs to the southwest corner of the field to find the short trail leading to the observation tower. From here you can look out over the marsh and see wood ducks, buffleheads, pied-billed grebes, great blue herons, osprey, beaver, and perhaps moose and loons. Songbirds abound, and the trail through the fields gives a closer view of the wildflowers.

Only 1¼ miles down the road is the **Paradise Point Nature Center** (look sharp to find its small sign up high on the uphill side of the road). In addition to the trails through an unspoiled lakeshore of coniferous forest, the center includes hands-on exhibits, a library, bird-viewing area, and a fascinating audio-aided exhibit illustrating the various calls of the loon. A small shop sells nature guides, minerals, and nature-oriented gifts and activities. A full schedule of naturalist programs is offered, including a sunrise canoe trip. Before walking the trails, be sure to pick up a free copy of their visitors guide, with its well-written descriptions of the natural history and inhabitants of the area. The center is open weekends 10:00 A.M. to 4:00 P.M. in the spring and fall and daily 10:00 A.M. to 5:00 P.M. from the last week in June to Labor Day. There is no admission fee, but the Audubon Society, which operates the center, is always grateful for donations to help them continue their work of acquiring and protecting natural habitats. Write Audubon Society of New Hampshire, North Shore Road, East Hebron 03232 or call (603) 744–3516.

Going west from Hebron through Groton, a road leads to **Sculptured Rocks.** About a mile from the turnoff, watch for a signpost, although the sign may not be there during the off–season. You'll see a parking area on the left, and the chasm is on the right side of the road. The river here has carved its way under granite boulders, leaving only the crowns of some and forming giant potholes in others that appear to have been the work of a giant ice cream scoop. Below the bridge a trail leads past falls, pools, rocks in fantastic shapes, and huge moss-covered boulders, culminating in a sheer rock cliff on one side. Notice the full-grown trees on the side walls with their roots gripping the walls like fingers. Although there are a number of beautiful cascades and flumes in New Hampshire, many with potholes, this one is the most visually varied and interesting.

The back road through Groton and North Rumney is a seldom-traveled alternative to Route 3A. The town of Rumney sits off of Route 25, spread around a central common. Quilt enthusiasts should stop at the Calico Cupboard for fabrics, supplies, classes, and finished quilts and coverlets (603–786–9567).

Quincy Road, which goes off the far end of Rumney's village green, will take you to **The Quincy Bog.** Exactly 2 miles from the village green you will see a stone pillar on either side of a small road to the left. Down this road one tenth of a mile there is another left, which ends shortly at the bog entrance. Nature trails and a viewing deck offer a look at rare bog plants and an ecosystem different from those of shores and marshes. The best months to see the bog plants in bloom are May and June.

On the way to and from Quincy bog you will pass the most unusual **Town Pound** in the state. While pounds were usually made of four sturdy stone walls, forming a square, with a gate on one side, the townspeople of old Rumney took advantage of a geological feature as interesting as the pound itself. Huge boulders, which appear to have fallen from the cliffs above, lie in a great tumble. Two of them form protected cavelike areas, and two others form straight walls. By adding only one and one-half sides and a gate, the town had a fine enclosure for stray animals, one that even had shelter from rain and wind. Climb through the space in the center of the back and you'll find a trail through an arch formed by two huge boulders. You can climb farther and wander amid these granite giants. It's a fascinating combination of natural and human history. You'll see one wall of the pound directly across the road from the immense boulder that sits almost in the road.

Leaving Rumney on Main Street you will pass an extraordinary garden where visitors are welcome. **Mr. Jacquith's Garden** seems to be in bloom all the time, with a succession of flowers set in showy beds along the road. A place of visual delight, this work of one man rivals the loveliest show gardens anywhere. Although there is no admission fee, you'll see a box for donations to help with the expense of replacing plants, and you should add something to it. Up the road from the garden is a perennial-plant nursery run by Mr. Jacquith's son and daughter-in-law. They have a charming small perennial garden, and they sell herb and flower plants from their greenhouse. In the summer you can find fresh vegetables at their farmstand. Jacquith's Greenhouse is on Main Street in Rumney (no phone).

The road past these gardens leads to Stinson Lake, past the Mary Baker Eddy House. She lived here in the early 1860s and the house is open Tuesday through Saturday 10:00 A.M. to 5:00 P.M. May through October. From here a guide will also take you to another Eddy home in North Groton. The road, which turns to gravel, continues to climb through the woods. Watch for a waterfall to the left just as you cross a bridge. Farther on, as you top the ridge, you will have spectacular views into the White Mountain National Forest, just a teaser for the views you will have as you go farther north.

If your taste for travel doesn't run to dirt roads, you can go north from Rumney through the National Forest along Route 118 or take Route 25 to Plymouth, a short distance away. On the way to Plymouth you'll pass The **Crabapple Inn** Bed and Breakfast in a beautiful 1835 home of Federal architecture. As well restored inside as outside, the inn provides such luxuries as a canopied four-poster bed in a room whose private bathroom is large enough to be a guest room. Decanters of sherry in each room, handmade quilts, antique furnishings, mountain views, herb and perennial gardens, and the choice of an elegant dining room or a bricked terrace as a setting for breakfast are just a few of the extra touches here. The apple-cinnamon-nut muffins are only a side dish at a breakfast of herbed omelet, French toast, or blueberry pancakes with country sausage, but everyone remembers them the best. The rates are a little higher than at many bed and breakfast accommodations (they begin at $70.00 per couple), but this elegant and comfortable home is well worth the little extra cost. Write Crabapple Inn, RR 4, Box 1955, Plymouth 03264 or call (603) 536-4476.

You won't have an easy time finding The Backyard Trattoria in Plymouth, since it's down an alley and no one you ask seems to have heard of it. It's behind (and under) the Trolley Stop. It is open only Friday through Sunday from 5:00 to 9:00 P.M., but the menu is rich in Italian favorites and interesting chef's specials that change daily. While you are downtown, look into the Plymouth Theater. It's a quintessential art deco movie theater restored to its 1931 grandeur, with a stainless steel and copper curved ticket box and mahogany doors. For the best ice cream in town, served in generous portions, climb the stairs to Jamies, at the old Plymouth Inn on South Main Street. The barrage of video-game noise from the amusement parlor next door may drive you outside, but you can't beat the ice cream.

Off the Beaten Path in the Lakes and Foothills

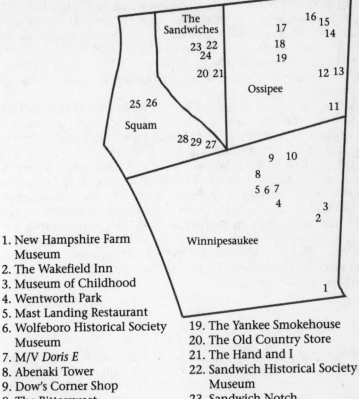

The Sandwiches

17
16 15
14
23 22
24
18
19
20 21
12 13
Ossipee
11
25 26
Squam
28 29 27
9 10
8
5 6 7
4
3
2
Winnipesaukee
1

1. New Hampshire Farm Museum
2. The Wakefield Inn
3. Museum of Childhood
4. Wentworth Park
5. Mast Landing Restaurant
6. Wolfeboro Historical Society Museum
7. M/V *Doris E*
8. Abenaki Tower
9. Dow's Corner Shop
10. The Bittersweet
11. The Effinghams
12. Freedom Historical Society
13. Fairfield Llama Farm
14. Purity Spring Resort
15. King Pine Ski Area
16. Madison Boulder
17. The Farm House
18. White Lake State Park
19. The Yankee Smokehouse
20. The Old Country Store
21. The Hand and I
22. Sandwich Historical Society Museum
23. Sandwich Notch
24. The Corner House
25. The Sailing Center
26. Science Center of New Hampshire
27. Centre Harbor Children's Museum
28. Red Hill Inn
29. Red Hill Ski Touring Center

The Lakes and Foothills

North of the Merrimack Valley and the seacoast regions lies an area of rolling farmlands and small mountains. The northernmost of these become the foothills of the White Mountains beyond.

In the center lies Lake Winnipesaukee, an enormous body of water surrounded by several other sizable lakes. The southern shores of Winnipesaukee are covered with popular tourist paths and filled with man-made "attractions" and cheek-by-jowl resorts. While there are some lovely, quiet pockets in this area, it is generally too well known and too heavily trodden to be of interest in this book.

Instead, we shall explore the eastern shore and other lakes east of I-91 and the mountains and forests that border them. Ossipee, Wentworth, Squam, Silver, and Province lakes are joined by innumerable smaller ones providing reflecting pools for some of the state's prettiest villages. We won't name or take you past all of them, so you should explore the back roads to discover some for yourselves. Country inns, covered bridges, rock-lined brooks, and old farms lie along back roads here, and at the crossroads are villages that date from the earliest days of the colony. Through it runs a road whose original route was selected so that the royal governor could travel from his capital in Portsmouth or his summer place in Wolfeboro to Dartmouth College. Other routes in the state are just as historic.

Winnipesaukee

The three Gilmantons sit in a triangle amid small lakes and the rolling, wooded foothills of the Belknap Mountains. Gilmanton, at the intersection of Routes 107 and 140, is a cluster of fine early homes, with several outstanding examples of Federal architecture. Ralph Waldo Emerson studied at the academy in the center of the village; facing it is a large church and a tavern built in 1793. Half a mile south of the center on Route 107 is a well-preserved town pound built to detain stray animals.

Other memories of New Hampshire's early agriculture are displayed and used at the **New Hampshire Farm Museum** on Plummers Ridge, just north of Milton. Housed in the best-preserved series of connected farm buildings in the state (the house and barn are connected by a series of buildings and sheds to facilitate winter access and farm chores), the museum began as a simple collection of early implements. It is now a living historical farm, showing both early methods and the evolution of farming. In addition to the house and barns there are blacksmith and cobbler shops and a country store. Special weekend events illustrating farm life include days for herbs, crafts, and dairy farming. The second Saturday in August is the main event, Old Time Farm Day, with over sixty demonstrations of farming skills and crafts. Open Tuesday through Sunday from 10:00 A.M. through 4:00 P.M. from late June until Labor Day; weekends only in the fall. Admission $4.00 for adults and $1.00 for children. Write New Hampshire Farm Museum, Route 16, P.O. Box 644, Milton 03851 or call (603) 652–7840.

For most of the nineteenth century, Wakefield Corner was an important stop on the route north, but then it lost its position to Sanbornville's rail junction. Since then, it has stayed so close to its nineteenth-century appearance that the entire village has been named a historic district. Its white wooden houses sit in gracious fence-encircled yards, and features such as the hay scales and horse trough are still standing.

The innkeepers of **The Wakefield Inn** have prepared a booklet describing the architecture and the buildings, which they lend to their guests who wish to take a walking tour. That's only one of many reasons for staying at this three-and-one-half-story Federal-style inn. The rooms are large, airy, and beautifully decorated, all with private baths. The dining room is known in the area for its innovative menu and careful preparation of such dishes as chicken breast with cornbread stuffing, crab-stuffed filet of sole, shrimp in Grand Marnier, pasta primavera, and shrimp baked in puff pastry. The menu describes dishes in detail; the only problem is that the details sound so delicious that it makes selecting a dinner even more difficult. Historical features such as original window glass, a three-sided fireplace, and Indian shutters make the inn as interesting as it is hospitable. Lunch and dinner are served Thursday through Sunday in the winter and Tuesday through Sunday during the rest of the year. Winter package specials include meals and such extras as cross-country skiing, quilting lessons, and sleigh rides. Write The Wakefield Inn at Mt. Laurel Road, Route 1, Box 2185, Wakefield 03872; call (603) 522–8272.

A few doors up the street is the newly opened **Museum of**

Childhood. Two sisters, Marjorie Banks and Elizabeth MacRury, have collected dolls and toys both at home and on their frequent foreign travels. When the collection threatened to engulf their home, they purchased a house a few doors away, and the museum was born. More than 2,000 dolls, from puppets to clothes-pin dolls, inhabit the rooms, along with teddy bears, sleds, and a *complete* 1890s schoolroom. The collectors, who are happy to accompany visitors and bring these bits of memories of childhood alive, are as delightful as the collection. Everyone leaves smiling, especially children, who can't resist the stories. "Sara is visiting her grandmother in Tuftonboro today, but she won't mind your looking in her room," Elizabeth assures a young visitor. Open May through October, Wednesday through Monday 11:00 A.M. to 4:00 P.M., except Sunday 1:00 P.M. to 4:00 P.M. The Museum of Childhood is on Mt. Laurel Road in Wakefield; call (603) 522–8073 for more information.

Despite all the lakes around, finding a public place to swim can be difficult. **Wentworth Park** on Route 109 between Wakefield and Wolfeboro is a small beach with bathhouses and a picnic area along its sandy shorefront. Nearby is the stone foundation and well of the summer estate of Benning Wentworth, first of New Hampshire's royal governors. This 100-foot by 40-foot structure with stories 18 feet high and windows 6 feet tall is thought to have been the first summer vacation "cottage" in America, built in 1768. Unfortunately, the estate burned not long after the Revolution. In the summer there is often an archeological dig here.

Wolfeboro is quite different from the towns along the southwestern shore of Lake Winnipesaukee. Its Main Street is busy in the summer, but there is a much more leisurely air here, with no traffic jams and honking horns. For a good lunch in a local, friendly atmosphere, stop at the **Mast Landing Restaurant** at the bridge in the middle of town. It's a classic, with blue painted booths, waitresses who chat with you, and daily specials on a bulletin board over the pie case (apple, blueberry, pumpkin, apricot, cherry, lemon meringue, and chocolate custard). It's not the place for an intimate tête-à-tête, but it's lively, friendly, and reliable. Open daily until 3:00 P.M. for breakfast and lunch only; breakfast is served all day. Call ahead for take-out lunches (603–569–1789).

The candy store next door has truffles, and across the street, New England Craftsmen has a nice selection of pewter jewelry and other locally crafted gifts and furnishings (603–569–5804). In the winter, North Country Skier on North Main Street offers 20 kilometers of well-groomed trails with lake views. This complete center offers equipment rentals and lessons as well as rental of ice skates to use on Perry Hollow Pond (603–569–3151).

Admission is free at the **Wolfeboro Historical Society Museum,** a collection of buildings that includes a mid-nineteenth-century firehouse, an 1820 schoolhouse, and an eighteenth-century home. Open Monday through Saturday 10:00 A.M. to 4:30 P.M. from July first to Labor Day on South Main Street in Wolfeboro; call (603) 569–4997. An interesting two-hour cruise of the islands on the east side of Lake Winnipesaukee leaves from Wolfeboro on Saturdays and Sundays at 10:00 A.M., 12:00 noon, and 2:00 P.M. or Friday and Saturday evenings at 6:30 P.M. The captain of the **M/V Doris E** points out interesting features on shore and enlivens the cruise with local stories and history. Light refreshments are available, but if you would like to enjoy a glass of wine with the sunset, you'll have to bring your own. The fare is $8.00 for adults and $4.00 for children. For details call (603) 366–2628.

New Hampshire has a number of museums based upon private collections. One such place is the imposing Libby Museum on Route 109 in Winter Harbor. From stuffed birds and fish to local Indian relics, the museum reflects the interests of the man who built it. There are even artifacts excavated from the Wentworth mansion. Open Memorial Day to Labor Day 10:00 A.M. to 4:00 P.M. except Mondays (603–569–1035). Across the road is a public boat launch; you can leave your car and boat trailer in the public parking lot behind the museum.

The **Abenaki Tower,** a little farther along Route 109 in Melvin Village, gives no clue to its origin except the date of its construction. This sturdy wooden structure puts you above the treetops for a 180-degree view over Lake Winnipesaukee and its wooded islands and many bays. The Belknap Mountains back it to the south and the Squam Range to the north. It's a short easy walk and then a stiff climb, but the view is spectacular, especially at sunset. Notice the unusual raised lines on the boulder near the trail.

Although there are antique shops all over the state, some of which come and go within a season or two, there is one in Tuftonboro that is well worth a visit. The **Dow's Corner Shop** has occupied its enormous barn for close to fifty years. It is so full of antiques that you have to walk sideways in the narrow aisles. From export china to 1920s fur coats, if you collect it, they'll not only have it, but they will have several to choose from. This is also a good place to find the once popular Kilburn stereoscopic view cards of New Hampshire. Open daily May 1 to October 15 and by chance in the winter. Dow's Corner Shop is on Route 171 at Tuftonboro Corner, R.F.D. Ossippee 03864; (603–539–4790).

Not far from there, on Route 28 in Wolfeboro, is **The Bitter-sweet,** whose barn dining room is decorated with utensils, implements, pottery, china, quilts, and old sheet music from area antique stores. All of these are for sale, with discreet price tags affixed. The interesting decor should not take your attention away from the menu, which presents a lively collection of entrees including duckling with raspberry, lamb and cider pie, herbed shrimp and vegetable stir-fry, Wiener schnitzel, and chicken piccata. Whatever you choose, don't miss the spinach salad with vinaigrette dressing. One word of warning, however, if you go on Friday or Saturday evening: Plan to be finished by 8:00 P.M. or expect to have your dinner table conversation drowned out by the percussion from the dance band in the pub downstairs. Open May to December, serving dinner Monday through Saturday, 5:00 P.M. to 9:00 P.M., and Sunday brunch buffet, 11:00 A.M. to 2:00 P.M. (603–569–3636).

Ossipee

Unlike New Hampshire's western border, where the Connecticut River makes a clean separation with Vermont, the border with Maine, north of Wakefield, is merely a surveyor's line. Roads and villages that grew up prior to this line sprawl and meander from one side to the other. Route 153 is one of these, not only a lovely road to travel, but a good alternative for shunpikers seeking to avoid the traffic of Route 16. On its way to Conway, this road weaves through valleys and around the shores of little lakes. Province Lake nudges it over the line into Maine for a few miles and it re-enters New Hampshire at South Effingham.

The Effinghams, and there are four of them, were once a very prosperous community based on a group of mills built along the Ossipee River in the 1820s. Center Effingham overlooks the road from a hill, with an imposing town hall that doubles as a Masonic

Lodge. That accounts for the emblem on the clock face. Almost in the shadow of its Italianate tower is Buttermilk Farm, a bed and breakfast in an 1832 stagecoach inn. These two, plus a grange hall, a church, and several homes complete the historic village.

To the north is Effingham, also known as Lord's Hill. This cluster of early nineteenth-century buildings includes a church, a 1780s hip-roofed house, and several impressive homes of 1820s origin. Just down from the crest of the hill is a road with a historic marker describing the Effingham Union Academy, New Hampshire's first state teachers college. A short distance up that road, set among manicured lawns and huge shade trees, is Squire Lord's mansion. For its size, and the quality of its architecture, this would be an impressive building in Portsmouth or Exeter. Here, come upon suddenly in such a rural setting, it is astonishing. Its three stories rise in clean lines, the eye drawn upward to the tall, octagonal, domed cupola. A Palladian window in the second floor surmounts the wide Federal doorway.

No longer open for public tours, the mansion is now a private home. Please respect this and continue down the road a few yards to the academy to turn around.

The town of Freedom lies along a small river, its two streets lined by fine homes, many with interesting decorative trim. On Maple Street is the **Freedom Historical Society,** whose collections include furnished rooms. The Victorian parlor is particularly illustrative of life in these prosperous mill towns during their heyday, with its ornate fainting couch and stereoscope viewer. Open Tuesday, Thursday, Saturday, and Sunday, 2:00 to 4:00 P.M. Just down the street is the Freedom House Bed and Breakfast, in a beautifully restored Victorian home. The guest rooms are bright and spotless with nice decorative detail. It is open year-round, and you'll have to reserve early to stay there during the town's annual Old Home Week in August. Write Freedom House Bed and Breakfast, Maple Street, Freedom 03836; call (603) 539–4815.

Fairfield Llama Farm, which you would expect to find in the surrounding farmland, is along the main street at a large townhouse. In the wide, sloping backyard live a small herd of the shaggy, irresistible creatures, their faces set in a perpetual grin. Deborah Frock will take you on leisurely treks with llamas carrying your lunch, cameras, and nature guides. The soft foot of the llama does no harm to woodlands, and hiking with one alerts you to the many pleasures of the forest. Deborah's favorite trek is to the summit of Foss Mountain, where there is a 360-degree view of Maine and New Hampshire as far as Mount Washington. This half-day trip can be made late in the day, in time to enjoy dessert, along with the sunset, at the summit and be back by dark. Write for reservations (she'll call you to confirm) at P.O. Box 96, Freedom 03836.

If you're staying at **Purity Spring Resort,** they'll pack an elegant dessert for you to carry along. But be sure to check their evening schedule, since you don't want to miss their Thursday evening lobster and steak cookout on their private island. Each day at this casual family resort brings new activities, from a Monday morning breakfast cookout with bacon, sausage, eggs, and toast cooked over the fire to the Friday night steamship smorgasbord. The dining room in the old-fashioned American-plan resort

Fairfield Llama Farm, Freedom

offers a choice of five entrees each evening, always including a meatless alternative. Meals aren't restricted to guests either, in case you are staying in a neighboring bed and breakfast—some local families come every week for the lobster cookout.

Everything here is included: day care for children, tennis, canoes, rowboats, and all activities. There are grandparents here who first came as children and have been returning ever since. It's not fancy, but it's very comfortable, with a homelike atmosphere. The spring for which it is named is in a little springhouse across the street, next to an old-fashioned up-and-down sawmill that the owners are in the process of restoring. Write Purity Spring Resort, East Madison 03849; call (800) 367–8897, in New Hampshire (603) 367–8896.

King Pine Ski Area is small, but it has trails at all skill levels. Four trails and the main slope are lighted for night skiing. Facilities are up to date, but prices are old-fashioned and made even better with ski-lodging packages at Purity Spring. A complete ski school and the relaxed atmosphere of King Pine make it a particular favorite of families. It's located in East Madison; call (603) 367–8896.

The **Madison Boulder,** off Route 113 between Conway and Madison, is the largest known example of a glacial erratic in New England, and one of the largest in the world. Enormous free-standing boulders are not uncommon in New Hampshire, but none even approaches the size of this 83-foot, 5,000-ton giant. This is not just another big rock. Such erratics were broken from large outcrops of granite by glaciers, carried away and dropped in spots sometimes several miles distant. This one is thought to have come from cliffs about 4 miles away, but some geologists believe that it came from Mount Willard, 25 miles north in Crawford Notch.

Just west of the intersection of Route 113 with Route 16 in Chocorua Village, you'll see **The Farm House** bed and breakfast. This bright and beautifully kept home is among the most hospitable lodgings in New England. Guests are welcomed with tea and homemade cookies or luscious chewy brownies served on the porch (or by the fire if it's frosty out). Breakfasts are elegantly served, using eggs and maple syrup from the farm. In March, though the inn isn't open to guests, you can watch a real sugar bush in operation as the Dyrenforths tap trees and boil sap into syrup in their sugarhouse. (Visitors are welcome to assist the innkeepers with maple-sugaring.) The muffins and breads here are exceptional. Open May through October. Write The Farm House, Chocorua Village 03817 or call (603) 323–8707.

White Lake State Park packs three attractions into one compact park that surrounds a crystal-clear lake. The lake's swimming beach stretches along one end, with the rest of the shore bordered in trees. A walking trail encircles its perimeter, and a campground with well-spaced sites is set under tall pine trees. Sites are large and open with their forest floor padded by a soft carpet of pine needles. Across the lake is a stand of pitch pines that have been declared a National Natural Landmark. Close to the northern tip of their range, the pitch pines here are especially large, which indicates age, but they are hard to date because they don't grow even rings for each year's growth. Pitch pine trees have difficulty reproducing except after a forest fire, since their cones need the heat to spring them open and release the seeds. Open from the end of May to Columbus Day, White Lake is in Tamworth; call (603) 323–7350.

Another interesting pine-forest environment is located a short distance away along the road between Silver Lake and West Ossipee. The West Branch Pine Barrens, part of which is owned by the Nature Conservancy, is considered one of the world's finest examples of pine barrens. Its layer of birch and scrub oak grows under a canopy of pitch pine, with blueberry bushes closer to the ground. The barrens is home to several rare moth varieties that feed on its trees.

Don't be put off by the picnic tables on the porch or by the fear of looking like the two fat pink pigs on the sign of **The Yankee Smokehouse** at the intersection of Routes 16 and 25 in West Ossipee. If you can, sit in the back dining room, which is really a sun porch decorated with stern portraits of someone's grandparents and the portrait of the boys and staff from some long-forgotten summer camp. The service is so unremittingly cheerful and eager here that it reminds us of Disney World. Servers describe each specialty and suggest the best deal. "You'll get more of the same thing for less money by ordering the sampler for one and splitting it," our waiter once advised us after mentally toting up our order. Beef or pork ribs or slices, chicken, and delicious baby back pork ribs are their specialties, but you can have the sliced smoked beef or pork cold in a sandwich or the chicken made into a wonderfully smoked salad. Don't miss the corn chowder (it's unlikely that your waiter will allow you to order a meal without it), which is solid with chunks of potato, bacon, and corn and seasoned with herbs and plenty of pepper, with a dash of Hungarian paprika for character. You can roll up your sleeves and eat until you can't hold another bite here and have trouble making the bill come out to $10.00 each. If you have a group of at least eight, order the Smokehouse Feast for $47.95. It says on the menu that it feeds four to six, but it's enough for a regiment on the march. Open all year except April and from mid-November to mid-December (603–539–RIBS).

The Sandwiches

Some of New Hampshire's quirky private museums—collections gathered over the years by people with a particular hobby or interest—have signs by the roadside inviting people in and some don't. Even when you're in **The Old Country Store** at the crossroads in Moultonboro, you might not notice the sign by the stairs pointing to the museum. The whole upper floor is filled with local history—saws, axes, and other tools; a wooden snow shovel; blacksmithing tools; maple sugaring equipment; advertising cards; cigar store Indians; yarn winders—neatly labeled and often in some detail. There is no curator and no charge; you just wander around at your leisure. You might want to show your appreciation by taking home some common crackers or some cheddar cheese from the wheel in the glass case downstairs or stopping for a Moxie or a cream soda from the big old ice chest, but everybody's very pleasant even if you don't. Outside in the barn is an original Concord Coach that is thought to be the oldest Concord-built stagecoach in existence.

Diagonally across the four corners is **The Hand and I,** a unique craft and woodworking school. Some craftspeople come just to use the tools, and others come to learn how at the morning and evening classes. Most of these run in two-week series, but special all-day classes or shorter sessions can be arranged. Subjects include weaving, pewter casting, box making, chair caning, origami, antique restoration, spinning, and other arts. Free demonstrations on a variety of craft-related subjects are offered the second Saturday of each month at 10:00 A.M. and 2:00 P.M. Fine craft tools and materials are sold here as well. Visitors are welcome to stop by and see the studios from 9:00 A.M. to 5:00 P.M. Monday through Saturday and 10:00 A.M. to 5:00 P.M. Sunday. Write The Hand and I, P.O. Box 264, Route 25, Moultonboro 03254 or call (603) 476–5121.

A good restaurant nearby is The Sweetwater Inn on Route 25, where they serve moderately priced northern Italian specialties such as fettucini with shrimp and scallops in a Dijon sauce, ravioli filled with lobster, veal medallions with assorted mushrooms, and chicken with shrimp and a hazel nut liqueur (603–476–5079).

The Woodshed, in a nicely adapted 1860s barn, is locally known for its beef, also at moderate prices. It's on Lee's Mill Road in Moultonboro (603–476–2311).

The Village of Center Sandwich is largely made up of houses built in the first half of the nineteenth century. The streets are lined with trees, and the houses clustered into a handful of streets, an open invitation to stroll through town. Along with the antique and craft shops, be sure to stop at the **Sandwich Historical Society Museum.** Its furnishings include a kitchen, household implements, and a wide variety of artifacts from the town's eighteenth-century beginnings through the early twentieth century. Open, free of charge, Monday through Saturday, 11:00 A.M. to 5:00 P.M. in July and August and 1:00 to 5:00 P.M. June and September (603–284–6665).

Follow Grove Street and then bear left at road signs for **Sandwich Notch.** It is reached by a gravel road that is not maintained for winter use. The stone walls beside it once outlined the fields of farms, now overgrown into forests. Once a cart track, the road was put through the notch in 1801 as a route for north-country farmers to get their produce to the markets of Portsmouth and Portland and return with supplies and goods not produced on their own farms. Later bypassed by other routes, the road through this notch has not changed very much for the past century and a half.

A parking area on the right, somewhat below the level of the road, marks the short trail to Beede's Falls. This is a place worth exploring. Where the trail meets the river, an island cuts the river into two small channels. To the right, the water slides over ledges and drops in a series of cascades into a moss-lined pool below. The wooded area at the bottom is surrounded by a tumble of boulders, some of which form caves and crevices. If you go upstream along the island, you will see the brook rushing through a foot-wide shoot. A short distance above that, the river flows down a ledge and then drops 40 feet into a sandy pool. More rocks lie in giant tumbles here, too. Some of these overhang enough to form a cave that, legend has it, sheltered a stray cow for an entire winter. Above the main falls there are two more cascades. Because there are no signs here, it would be easy to miss the main falls to the left and to assume the cascades downstream to be Beede's Falls.

Not far up the road, between two bridges over the Bearcamp River, is a cliff shaped like the prow of a ship. Called Pulpit Rock, it was used as a pulpit by a long-ago Quaker pastor. The rocks behind this are interesting to explore, and the flat spot by the river makes a lovely, cool place to have a picnic. The head of the notch, 7 miles from the center of Center Sandwich Village, is marked by a small sign high up on a tree and not easy to see. For a well-written history of the notch, read *The Road Through Sandwich Notch* by Elizabeth Yates. (See book list, p. 138.)

There are more entrees on the daily special blackboard at **The Corner House** in Center Sandwich than most restaurants have on their printed menu. These dishes allow the chef to take advantage of ingredients with short seasons or those that are rarely available; they also give him the chance to serve his latest original dish. This might be a double lamb chop stuffed with a blend of ricotta, parmesan, and spinach. The printed menu is certainly not ho-hum, with such offerings as medallions of chicken breast stuffed with ham and artichoke hearts or veal smothered in chunks of lobster with broccoli and béarnaise sauce or the shellfish sautéed with sherry. Desserts change daily, and the descriptions delivered tableside are rich enough. Chambord cheesecake, crepes with ice cream, Kahlua chocolate cake, Mississippi mud brownies, and strawberry shortcake are just a sampling. A grinding of nutmeg on the cappuccino tops off a fine dinner here. Prices are moderate; lunch is served (try the crabcakes) every day except Sunday in the summer and on Wednesday through Saturday in the winter. Dinner is served every summer evening from 5:30 P.M. and Wednesday through Sunday in the winter.

Upstairs there are four guest rooms decorated with a stylish Victorian flair and moderately priced. Furnishings include brass and oak beds, wicker chairs, hand-hooked rugs, spool towel racks, marble-topped bureaus, and prints that range from Godey's *Lady's Book* to French Impressionist exhibition posters. Open year-round; write The Corner House, Box 204, Center Sandwich 03227 or call (603) 284–6219.

Several covered bridges are located along roads that wind among the hills and lakes here. Ask your innkeepers for directions or just drive around the area and look for the small road signs picturing covered bridges. Most of New Hampshire's covered bridges are on side roads that have been bypassed by other routes.

Squam

The quiet of Squam Lake is almost legendary. Its irregular shape, with bays, inlets, and islands, makes it virtually impossible for power boats to get up any speed, so there is very little to disturb the loons that nest there. Cottages along the shore are tucked behind the trees, giving it the feel of a wilderness lake. See it from the water in a canoe or sailboat rented at **The Sailing Center** on Route 3 in Holderness. They offer Phantoms, Daysailers, Hobies, and 16-foot fiberglass canoes, complete with all safety equipment, as well as sailing lessons. Rates run from $15.00 for half-day canoe rental to $55.00 for a 17-foot Daysailer. Full-day and weekly rentals bring the rates even lower. Call (603) 968–3233 to reserve a craft.

The **Science Center of New Hampshire** encourages visitors to explore six different natural communities along its exhibit trail. Signs, exhibits, and staff members explain the ecosystems of the marsh, field, pond, stream, forest, and lake, showing how plants and animals live together in each setting. Signboards explore such questions as "If the marsh were drained, who would suffer?" The marsh community is reached by a boardwalk, often covered with little bodies lying on their stomachs watching painted turtles, leopard frogs, trout, or other creatures below. Birds are everywhere, perched on fences or signposts, darting between trees, or chirping at eye level from branches on marsh shrubs. The setting is lovely and well maintained, a good way to understand the woods, fields, and waters that surround you as you travel throughout the state. Admission during July and August is $4.00 for adults and $2.00 for children. In May, June, September, and October it drops to $2.00 and $1.00. Summer hours are daily 9:30 A.M. to 4:30 P.M.; spring and fall hours are the same on weekdays but 1:00 to 4:00 P.M. on Saturdays and Sundays. Write P.O. Box 173, Route 113, Holderness 03245; call (603) 968–7194.

Although Center Harbor is at the very tip of Lake Winnipesaukee, its atmosphere is more akin to the quiet of Squam Lake. Why, you may ask, is a harbor at the far end of the lake named "Center Harbor"? The answer is that it was originally "Senter Harbor" after Colonel Joseph Senter, who was given the land by the king as thanks for his services during the French and Indian War. To confuse us even further, several businesses there spell it "Centre," but the state highway map spells it "Center" and so shall we.

The **Centre Harbor Children's Museum** is not just for rainy days. Its interactive displays and activities are for toddlers through younger teens (and older teens if they have a younger guest as an excuse). In the bubble room they can enclose themselves in a giant bubble or create unusual shapes in enormous trays of soapy solution. Next door, kids can build a log cabin, and in the music room they can play instruments in little sound booths. Costumes, puppets, books, the wheelhouse of a ship, and other activities are good for hours of fun. If you go in the morning, you're welcome to return after lunch; your admission is good for the entire day. A small museum shop is packed with craft materials, science and educational toys, and games for all ages. Open every day in July and August from 9:00 A.M. to 8:00 P.M.; winter hours are Wednesday through Friday, 9:00 A.M. to 3:00 P.M., Saturday, 10:00 A.M. to 5:00 P.M., and Sunday, 11:00 A.M. to 5:00 P.M. Admission is $4.00 each, babies under one year free. Write P.O. Box 1537, Center Harbor 03226 or call (603) 253–TOYS.

Between visits, parents can browse in Holiday House Antiques across the road or in the quilt shop next door.

In 1904, the heir of the man who invented and manufactured the soda fountain built a brick summer home in Center Harbor overlooking Squam Lake and the Squam mountain range. Unlike many northern homes, it had wide hallways, huge windows, and other elements of southern architecture; it was a showplace, even in an area rich in opulent private estates. It passed from his family through several owners, including minor European royalty, and eventually became Belknap College. When the college failed in the mid-1970s, the house remained empty and soon fell prey to vandals who stripped it of even its copper wiring. Weather continued the destruction until the house was finally scheduled for burning.

In 1985 its present owners bought it and immediately began to restore and refurnish it to its original style. The result is a period-piece mansion that visitors would gladly pay admission to tour.

Red Hill Inn is both lodging and restaurant, and it does both equally well. Despite its Victorian air, the relaxed feeling of a vacation home is still strong. Enormous guest rooms and suites are bright and airy with spectacular views over lawns, gardens, and the estate's farmhouse and barns to Squam Lake and the mountains beyond. In the evenings from the front rooms, dining room, and terrace, you can watch the setting sun turn the sky and lake to gold, the lawn to a brighter green, and the facing mountainsides dark with long shadows.

The food will demand your attention, even with the view for competition. Begin with a stuffed onion, half a giant Spanish onion filled with artichoke hearts and aged cheddar, and then work your way through a soup bowl of salad, lively with a tangy but not overpowering Dijon and chutney dressing. The milk-fed veal, fork tender, is in a caper sauce with tiny spring potatoes, and young tender rabbit is served with a shallot brown sauce. Desserts are just as original: apricot pie, Kentucky High (with bourbon and chocolate), English lemon pound cake with orange sherbet and a custard sauce, and two old-time Yankee specialties—Indian pudding and vinegar pie. That's one you won't have a chance to try anywhere else. Cappuccino and espresso are offered, along with a nice selection of teas. Menu prices are moderate.

Don't miss the lounge at the opposite end of the inn from the dining room. The bar is half of a wooden hulled Cris Craft that one of the owners bought after an accident had ruined the other side. The entire inn is decorated with the owners' collections, including several groups of early cameras.

In the summer, guests can hike to tiny secluded beaches on Squam's shores, where the bottom is sandy and the water shallow enough for children to splash in safety for quite a distance. Rates for rooms and suites in the inn and the adjacent farmhouse vary with size and location, from $65.00 to $105.00 including a generous country breakfast. Write Red Hill Inn, Box 99M, Center Harbor 03226; call (603) 279–7001.

Winter visitors to the Squam area can enjoy cross-country skiing free of charge at the **Red Hill Ski Touring Center** on Route 25B in Center Harbor. Intermediate- and beginner-level trails lead along the hillside meadows, through the woods, and along the shores of the lake. Rental ski equipment is available at Red Hill Inn.

Ashland, at the geographical center of New Hampshire, is home to the state's newest covered bridge spanning the Squam River, just at the shore of Little Squam Lake. Located just off the road to Holderness, the bridge was locally built and was hauled into place by a local team of oxen. The Common Man Deli is a good place to assemble a picnic lunch for your canoe trips or meanderings through the countryside.

Off the Beaten Path in the Eastern White Mountains

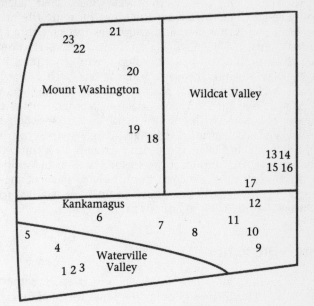

1. The Cascades
2. The Coffee Emporium
3. The Snowy Owl
4. Thornton Gap
5. Russell Pond Campground
6. Kancamagus Pass
7. Sabbaday Falls
8. Rail 'n River Forest Trail
9. Indian Museum
10. Cathedral Ledge
11. Diana's Baths
12. Abenaki Encampment and Shop
13. Wentworth Resort
14. Jackson Falls
15. Jackson Ski Touring Foundation
16. Inn at Jackson
17. Grand Manor Antique and Classic Car Museum
18. Crawford Notch
19. Livermore
20. Mount Willard
21. Jefferson Notch
22. Zealand Falls
23. Sugarloaf Campground

The Eastern White Mountains

The White Mountains are the stuff of Indian legend and settlers' folk tales, of larger-than-life explorers and pioneers. Until the discovery of Crawford Notch, they presented a barrier that kept the lands to the north in isolation.

In the nineteenth century they were "discovered" again, this time by wealthy families from the cities escaping the heat and dust. With maids, nannies, and enormous trunks, entire families boarded trains in New York, New Haven, Boston, Hartford, and other cities bound for Jackson, Glen, Twin Mountain, Bretton Woods, Dixville, and Crawford. Some hotels, such as the Mount Pleasant, had porticoes that reached out over the railroad tracks. Others sent elegant Concord Coaches, resplendent in canary yellow or cherry red with gold-leaf scrollwork, to welcome guests. They stayed all summer, hiking, riding, swimming (called "bathing"), playing lawn sports, and dancing to a full orchestra every evening. This annual social season lasted until World War II and the invention of air conditioning. Now most of the grand hotels are gone, but the few that remain have retained the fine traditions that made them famous in their golden age.

Waterville Valley

The Waterville Valley is a cul-de-sac cut deep into the White Mountain National Forest. Route 49 follows the Mad River, which is really quite benign except in the spring when it carries the runoff from a vast watershed and pours it into the Pemigewasset River. After 12 miles of narrow wooded passage, the valley opens suddenly into a broad floor of fields and a resort village reminiscent of Alpine ski towns.

While it's best known for its ski area, that's usually bypassed for the taller mountains to the north and closer to I-93. But Waterville is a favorite of families who feel perfectly safe letting their children travel between slopes and lodging in this isolated and hometown atmosphere. Its children's ski school has an area all of its own and is considered one of the nation's best places for children to learn to ski. Although Waterville is small, its facilities are state of the art and waits for lifts up Mount Tecumseh are rare indeed.

One of New Hampshire's oldest resort areas—the first hotel was built here in the 1860s—its location has always protected it from becoming too big. By 1900 there was a golf course here, but hiking and fishing were the favorite activities of early vacationers. There are 22 miles of hiking trails and several mountain summits whose trails begin in the valley. One of the shorter trails for more casual hiking begins at the bottom of the Snow's Mountain ski lift and leads to **The Cascades.**

Follow the signs, climbing up the ski slope and then to the left. Be sure that you are following the Cascades signs and *not* the Snow's Mountain cross-country ski trail. Once you are in the woods, look for yellow trail blazes. There are very few steep places on this easy trail through the woods. Once you get to the cascades, cross the brook and continue up the other side for the best views of the continuous series of waterfalls and pools.

As you can tell from the many trail signs, in the winter the valley and its hillsides are a web of cross-country ski trails. There is an excellent trail map available free at the cross-country ski center in Town Square. Use it to determine the steepness or difficulty of a particular trail before beginning an outing.

Après ski, après hike, or any other time, stop at **The Coffee Emporium** at the Town Square for a mind-boggling selection of twenty-two fine coffees fresh ground and brewed, served in generous amounts. Along with cappuccino, espresso, cafe au lait, and a chocolate-topped specialty, they have hot chocolate in both brown and white, served with whipped cream. They also have a fine selection of teas. There's an assortment of pastries and desserts as well as Belgian waffles with your choice of toppings and other daily breakfast specials. Coffee by the pound, fine teas, and coffee mugs are sold as well. Open 8:00 A.M. to 9:00 P.M. every day (603–236–4021).

OK, we admit it: We like the trappings of luxury, and our favorite place to stay in the valley is **The Snowy Owl.** Summer or winter, its three-story-tall fieldstone fireplace identifies it as a ski lodge. In the big downstairs lounge area, a sunken pit provides guests a place to gather by the fire in the evening. In the afternoon, wine and cheese await returning hikers and skiers. Rooms are spacious; especially nice are the upper-level rooms with loft bunks for the kids. In-suite whirlpool baths, an indoor swimming pool, and a kids-stay-free policy make this newly built inn an old-fashioned value. Call (603) 236–8383 or (800)

258–8988 for information and reservations, and be sure to ask about their money-saving seasonal packages.

Except in winter, when the road is closed, a nice alternative route out of the valley is over **Thornton Gap.** This small notch is reached from a road to the left at the village library. Follow signs to Tripoli (pronounced "triple-eye") Road, a fern-lined gravel byway that follows a mountain brook through the forest.

After you crest the gap, you drop down into the Pemigewasset valley near **Russell Pond Campground.** For those who enjoy camping as a sport, not simply as a way to reduce lodging costs, this National Forest campground is a gem. Sites are well separated, deep in a hardwood forest that drops into a lovely small pond. No buildings mar its shore; there is a canoe launch, a fisherman or two, and the deep quiet that only lakes that ban motor boats can offer. There are no showers at the campground and no RV hookups. It's hard to believe that such quiet wilderness can be so close to an interstate highway.

The Kancamagus

Only one road cuts directly east and west through the center section of the White Mountain National Forest—the Kancamagus Highway. Not really a highway, but a paved, two-lane road, it climbs from Lincoln to Conway over the 2,860-foot **Kancamagus Pass** via a long switchback. Be sure to stop at the pull-out areas to enjoy the view back across the mountains. One of these sits above the level of the highway and offers a panorama that you'll miss from the road. Once you reach the top of the pass, an entirely different panorama lies ahead, backed by the Presidential Range.

There is no commercial development along this entire route, just the woods, the views, small trailhead parking areas, and a handful of National Forest campgrounds. After descending, the other side the road is quite level all the way into Conway.

Watch the south side of the road for the sign for **Sabbaday Falls.** From the picnic area, the path is broad, smooth, and quite well marked to the foot of a flume, where the river flows through a 10-foot gap between straight rock walls more than 40 feet high. At the base there is a water-worn pothole about 4 feet in diameter, and nearby a 2-foot-wide stripe of dark basalt runs through the granite shelf that forms the viewing platform for the flume.

The trail along the rim is secured by a log railing, so you can safely look straight down into the chasm. Full-grown trees cling to the opposite wall, their roots like giant fingers gripping the rock.

The river comes spilling over the far side of the rim in a long unbroken falls. Above, a series of cascades and pools is formed by layers of overhanging ledge. You can see here very clearly the dramatic upstream march of the vertical wall of a waterfall. As potholes are formed by whirlpools, their walls are washed or worn away and the ledges are undercut.

About 3 miles east of the Sabbaday Falls trailhead is the George House, which is also known as the Russell-Colbath house. This 1805 farmhouse has been restored to the mid-nineteenth century, providing an interesting look at the isolated lives of the families who settled the Passaconaway Valley. The house is open daily 9:00 A.M. to 4:30 P.M. between mid-June and Labor Day and on weekends after Memorial Day and until Columbus Day in the fall.

Behind the house, **Rail 'n River Forest Trail** is a short (about a half mile), level loop that offers a unique view of the logging that once took place here and of the regrowth of the forest. Signboards and a free leaflet explain and show different kinds of forest environments, how timber was carried out of the valley by rail, and methods used to fight forest fires. The tale of the timbering that once stripped this entire area of its forests is now told only by ghosts, such as the pilings of a railroad bridge in the bed of the Swift River, visible from this trail, and by local place names such as Jigger Johnson and C. L. Graham Wangan. For a closer look at these rough-and-tumble days read *Tall Trees, Tough Men* by Robert E. Pike. (See book list, p. 138.) The trail is wheelchair accessible.

Close to the Rail 'n River Forest Trail is the turnoff for the paved road over Bear Notch, a steep, but good, road that shortens the trip to Bartlett and Crawford Notch to 9 miles, about one quarter of the distance of the route through Conway. Near the top is a scenic pull-out overlooking Mount Washington and the mountains to the north. Except for this view and another looking south toward Mount Chocorua, the road is closely bordered by forest. The road is not plowed in the winter.

If you decide not to take the Bear Notch road, shortly before the town of Conway and busy Route 16 you will reach Baldy's. This single building houses a small grocery store, an ice cream counter, an Indian souvenir shop, a snowshoe shop, and an **Indian Museum.** The last two are the reason for our stop. Treffle Bolduc

(Baldy) lived with the northern tribes and learned snowshoe making from them. You'll find his snowshoes all over northern New Hampshire, not only because they last, but because his prices are so reasonable that you can afford to outfit the whole family with snowshoes.

Indian lore has been a lifetime interest for Baldy, and he has gathered an astonishing collection of artifacts that includes stone projectiles, baskets, cornhusk masks, snowshoes, quill baskets, birchbark containers, beaded mukluks, soapstone carving, and a birchbark canoe. This is not a fancy museum, but rather a collector's treasure horde, displayed in two small rooms with about as much light as the inside of a tepee. But it's real and reflects one man's zeal to preserve and treasure a way of life that very few people have shared. Admission is only $2.00, and the museum is open from 2:00 to 5:00 P.M., except in the winter, when it closes at 4:00 P.M. The store is open longer hours, into the evening in the summer, so someone will probably let you into the museum at times other than its official hours. Call (603) 447–5287 or 356–7651 for information.

Route 16 from the northern end of Conway to above North Conway is so beaten a path that on summer and fall weekends the traffic may be backed up for hours. But there is a way around it, and it takes you past two delightful corners that people honking their horns on Route 16 never hear about. But first you have to find West Side Road.

Just opposite the intersection where Route 153 heads south to Eaton Center is a street going north. Take it and then the left at the fork (straight ahead is one of Conway's covered bridges, and to the left you will pass another one just a few yards up the road). Follow this road through lovely farmlands that open out to some of the valley's finest views of the Presidential Range.

You will eventually come to a point where the road comes to a **T**, at which point you should go left (the right would take you into North Conway). Down the road a short distance is a sign announcing **Cathedral Ledge,** which is the rock face that you have been getting glimpses of on your left. Follow that paved road, which becomes *very* steep as it climbs to the top of the cliff, and you will be treated to a view over Echo Lake and the entire valley as well as the ski trails carved on the face of Mount Cranmore on the opposite range of mountains. Sturdy steel fences protect you from a sudden unexpected descent. Our favorite time of day here is late in the afternoon when the shadows are long in the valley, but the sun hits squarely on the range of mountains to the east. Earlier in the day, if the weather is good, you can watch from below as rock climbers practice on the face of the ledge.

Less than a mile to the north, on the left of West Side Road, is the unmarked trailhead to **Diana's Baths.** Look for a wide, straight, gravel road, between two fenced fields, which ends abruptly at the edge of the woods. Only here will you finally find the signs identifying the trail.

The falls, only a half a mile along a fairly level trail, were once the site of a gristmill. You can still see the foundations and the chute that fed it water. Above, the falls alternate between falls and pools, interspersed with cascades over sloping granite. Each of these succeeding shelves is marked by potholes cut into its surface, like a series of children's marble holes in a school yard. As you continue to climb, either through the tumble of boulders that line the ledges or through the woods, you will find the ledges flatter and the falls shorter. But the swirls and scoops in the granite become even more dramatic.

In Intervale, back on the now calm Route 16, is a scenic overlook with a fine panorama of the mountains and Cathedral Ledge. Opposite is Intervale Crossroad, right beside the post office. Only about 100 yards up this road on your left, you will see a little cabin and a stone with a bronze plaque. Park and cross the railroad to the **Abenaki Encampment and Shop.** Each summer, from 1884 until 1964, members of the Abenaki tribe came from their winter home in Quebec to Cathedral Woods, where they camped and traded. This was during the Golden Age of the White Mountain hotels, and their guests used to enjoy visiting the encampment to watch the Abenaki weave baskets, which made fine souvenirs. Stephen Laurant, son of the Abenaki chief who started the encampment, still owns the property and the little shop that has been in use there since the late nineteenth century.

Go when you can spend some time to hear the stories of this Abenaki scholar, who is continuing his father's life work of writing a dictionary of the Abenaki language. Along with sweetgrass baskets, beadwork, and Nemadji earth pottery, there are publications on Indian culture for sale. An authentic birchbark tepee stands nearby under majestic pine trees. The shop is open daily from June 15 to October 15, 10:00 A.M. to noon and 3:00 to 5:00 P.M.

Abenaki Encampment, Intervale

Wildcat Valley

Tucked into a corner, away from the hustle to the south, is the lovely village of Jackson, with its red covered bridge and white church. Artists discovered it in the mid-1800s for its scenic beauty, and by the turn of the century, Jackson had twenty-four lodging places, including several grand hotels. By the late 1970s only Eagle Mountain House and a few smaller guest houses were still operating.

But this story has a happier ending than most. Today a number of these have reopened, including the Victorian treasure, Wentworth Hall. Not all of the original thirty-nine buildings could be saved from years of neglect and abandonment, but the three central ones and several other cottages with their curved porches, round towers, wide gables, and quirky architectural detail are once again the showpiece of the village center.

The **Wentworth Resort** is just as nice inside as outside, with real feather pillows, giant bathtubs, and a general air of grandeur that is comfortable, not intimidating. One of the Arden Cottage rooms has its own porch, a double Jacuzzi, and a window-lined sitting area formed by the base of the tower, and rooms in Wildwood Cottage are equally unique.

No matter how beautiful the rooms are, it's the dining room that everyone remembers the longest. The menu is unique and innovative, but not just for the sake of being different. Each season brings new dishes as the chef takes advantage of the freshest ingredients. Appetizers might be rosettes of smoked salmon on dill crepes or smoked duck breast on a bed of grilled red onions and spinach dressed with balsamic vinaigrette. The onion soup is laced with cider and cheddar, the veal topped with morels and brandy, the quail stuffed with wild rice and cashews, and the scallops sautéed with leeks in a creamy lobster sauce. A sunburst of shrimp alternating with avocado is served on a radiant puree of roasted sweet red peppers; vegetables are hot, herbed, crisp, and moist. Service is proper without being pompous, and the clientele is relaxed and informal. The public is invited to dine there but should call to make reservations. The hotel is open year-round. Write The Wentworth Resort Hotel, Box M, Jackson 03846; call (603) 383–9700 or (800) 637–0013.

A short walk up the road is **Jackson Falls,** a series of cascades with potholes that invite jumping in, if the weather is only

Wentworth Resort, Jackson

halfway nice. The hotel has a pool, of course, but these falls must have been the original inspiration for water slides. There is a circular route of 6 miles (called, for some reason, the Five Mile Drive) that begins at the Wentworth and goes up the Carter Notch Road past the falls. Instead of continuing to the top of the notch (where the road turns into a trail), turn right and cross the river. The views from this ridge across highland meadows to the mountains are lovely.

On the way up, the great white porches of Eagle Mountain House overlook the road. This is a good place to come on a weekend for their very reasonably priced breakfast buffet. A variety of fresh fruit, corned beef hash, French toast, homefries, bacon, sausage, eggs, Danish, and croissants are served in a classic, old, high-ceilinged dining room with deep green walls and huge windows. It's like stepping back to the early years of the century. They won't mind your sitting a spell on their porch and admiring the views after breakfast. Write The Eagle Mountain Resort, Carter Notch Road, Jackson, 03846 or call (603) 383–9111 or (800) 777–1700.

Black Mountain Ski Area is usually forgotten in the razzmatazz of its bigger neighbors, but it's a favorite of anyone who has ever skied there. Lines are shorter, the lodge friendly, and everyone a little more relaxed at this end-of-the-road slope. Trails are available at all levels, but most are in the intermediate range.

Cross-country skiing is an art form in Jackson. This is the home of the **Jackson Ski Touring Foundation,** which maintains 150 kilometers of exceptionally well-groomed trails throughout the village and all over the surrounding hillsides. In winter, with no leaves to obscure the view, the neighboring mountains, including the southern slopes of Mount Washington, are visible from every hillside. It's so beautiful on a crisp winter day that it's hard to concentrate on skiing.

You can ski right out the back door of the **Inn at Jackson,** and a shuttle bus will bring you home. This former summer "cottage," designed by the architect Stanford White, has eight enormous guest rooms with closets the size of bathrooms and bathrooms the size of bedrooms. Each group of rooms has a central living room, giving the feeling of staying in a private home. The fireplace on the first floor is a gathering place for all guests. Breakfast always features a specialty dish such as a quiche, French toast, or a delicious egg and cheddar bread pudding. Open all year-round. Write The Inn at Jackson, Thorn Hill Road, Jackson 03846; call (603) 383–4321 or (800) 289–8600.

The **Grand Manor Antique and Classic Car Museum** provides a constantly changing collection of cars from the Stanley Steamer (try to imagine Mr. and Mrs. Stanley driving up Mount Washington in this!) to the Edsel and the finned convertibles of the Fifties. In addition to the gleaming restored cars (one with glow-in-the-dark paint), there is a fire engine with its original gold leaf intact. Some of the cars are available for rental, others for sale, so if you see one you can't live without, you could end up driving it home. The attached gift shop is the perfect source of gifts for your favorite car buff, with old issues of motor magazines, original shop manuals, model cars, postcard replicas of old car ads, and a few other pieces including medals and insignia from both world wars. It's open daily in summer from

9:30 A.M. to 5:00 P.M., weekends only in the spring and fall. You'll find the museum on Route 16 in Glen (603-356–9366).

Mount Washington

At just over a mile high, Mount Washington is the highest mountain in the northeast, but its weather conditions are among the most severe in the world. Arctic equipment is tested at its summit. Only sightly below it stand other mountains named for presidents—thus the name "Presidential Range."

Crawford Notch, a break in the almost solid chain of the White Mountains, lies due south of Mount Washington. Geologically, the notch is a classic glacial scour. During the ice age, boulders frozen into the ice caught onto chunks of loose bedrock as the glacier moved down mountain slopes. In valleys, where the action of the glacier became more concentrated, the scouring was at its greatest, carrying off boulders and pieces of broken cliffs which in turn scraped even deeper as they moved, giving a characteristic **U**-shaped curve to the valley walls.

Now that we have roads and cleared fields, it is easy to see the shapes and silhouettes of these mountains, but in the early days of settlement, vast forests of very tall trees covered all but the tops of the mountains, so the settlers couldn't tell where the notches and the passes were. About all they could do was to follow the riverbeds, hoping to find the easiest and lowest route.

Usually, these routes were discovered more or less by accident. So it was with Timothy Nash the day he climbed a tree on Cherry Mountain while moose hunting and saw the gap in the line of mountains. He went to Portsmouth to ask the royal governor (the same Benning Wentworth that we met earlier) for a piece of land and a road through the notch. The governor told him to bring a horse through the notch, which Timothy and a friend did by lowering it over the cliff on a rope. Nash got his land, and eventually the road was built, opening a much shorter route to the north country.

The trees that filled the notch, like those of Passaconaway, fell to the lumber market. Entire towns sprang up around the lumber camps, and some of them died with the industry. **Livermore,** a ghost town today, lies along Sawyer River Road, which meets Route 302 just north of the bridge over the Sawyer River about 5 miles north of Bartlett. A mile and a half up Sawyer River Road you'll see a barred gate and some foundations, which are all that is left of Livermore. It was once a thriving community of 200, built in the late 1800s and reached by both road and railroad. Of its homes, stores, boarding houses, offices, and two saw mills, you'll find only ruins. Walk to the river and into the woods upstream to find cellar holes and the ruins of a beautifully constructed concrete and brick sawmill. All of these have full-sized trees growing out of them now. It's easier to find the cellar holes in the fall when the leaves are missing. Look for the one with the company safe clearly visible.

At the "head" of the notch is a narrow gateway and the old train station where the summer guests arrived, bound for the Crawford House Hotel, which once stood guard over the notch. The hotel is gone, but the little Victorian station is an Appalachian Mountain Club (AMC) information center, where you can get trail maps and advice if you plan to do any serious climbing.

If you plan to hike to Zealand Falls, be sure to pick up the free hiking sheet and map. Not only do these describe the trail features in detail, but they give fascinating information on the social and natural history of each area. The information is produced by the Forest Service, which maintains the White Mountain National Forest (within which this entire area lies).

The best view of Crawford Notch is down into it from **Mount Willard,** an easy climb (more accurately, an uphill walk) along an old bridle path to the summit. From there you can see the great scoop of the notch below you as well as the shimmering cascades that fall off the mountains through rocky ravines. Watch overhead for peregrine falcons, which have nesting sites near the summit of Mount Willard.

Past Echo Lake, which is the source of the Saco River, is Mount Clinton Road, which leads to **Jefferson Notch.** Possibly the least known of the White Mountain notches, its 3,009-foot elevation is the highest point in the state reached by a public road. Gravel all the way, the road passes through deep woods along Monroe Brook, which cascades over rocks between moss-covered banks. At the top, the forest is still too tall to allow any panoramic views, but drive into the parking lot for a good, close view of Mount Washington's summit, 3,000 feet above you. The road descends into the town of Jefferson; the entire trip is 9 miles.

Instead of leaving the area via Jefferson Notch, you can continue along Route 302 to the Zealand Campground, where there is a nice picnic area along the Ammonoosuc River. If you continue up the Zealand Road, about 3½ miles to its end, you can take the Zealand Trail to **Zealand Falls,** a 2½-mile, easy hike. Getting to the top of the falls is the only climbing involved—there is only about a 350-foot difference in altitude from the parking lot to the top of the falls. The falls is really a cascade, pleasant enough but not the reason for the hike. Atop the falls from the AMC hut is a view of New Hampshire's hidden notch. Only hikers can see the dramatic shape of Zealand Notch, for no road penetrates to it at any point. Take a lunch to eat by the falls as you enjoy the view. Along the trail you will follow the bed of a nineteenth-century logging railroad and pass through hardwood forests. It's hard to picture this entire valley laid waste by uncontrolled lumbering and the resulting fire and erosion damage, so great was the ability of the forest to rejuvenate itself here.

About halfway up the Zealand Road is the **Sugarloaf Campground,** one of the loveliest and most secluded in the mountains. Its sites are carved out of young forest, but most are roomy and sunny. Some have direct paths to the rocky Zealand River below. Resident hosts, a lively couple who have camped here for over thirty years, occupy a central campsite all summer and can tell you where the best fishing and blueberrying is. They have some wonderful tales to tell (some of them about us!). For information, write to the District Ranger, White Mountain National Forest, Bethlehem 03574.

Off the Beaten Path in the Western White Mountains

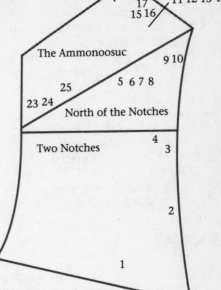

18 19 20 21
22
17
15 16
11 12 13 14

The Ammonoosuc

9 10

25
5 6 7 8

23 24

North of the Notches

4
3

Two Notches

2

1

1. Kinsman Notch
2. Cascade Brook and Kinsman Falls
3. New England Ski Museum
4. The Rim Trail
5. Harman's Store
6. Historical Museum
7. Hilltop Inn
8. North Country Chamber Players
9. The Franconia Marketplace
10. Robert Frost Place
11. The Mulburn Inn
12. The Bells
13. Rosa Flamingo's
14. Nanook Children's Wear
15. The Rocks
16. Maplewood
17. Newt Washburn
18. Bishop's Ice Cream Shoppe
19. Historical Museum
20. Littleton Stamp and Coin Company
21. Tim-Ber Alley
22. Moore Station Dam
23. The Brick Store
24. Bath Village Bridge
25. Upper Village

The Western White Mountains

The summer social season on this side of the White Mountains involved not only guests at the grand hotels—Profile House, Forest Hills, Sunset Hill, and the resorts of Bethlehem—but an increasing number of wealthy people who built their own summer estates, especially in Sugar Hill and Bethlehem. When the era of hotel summers ended, these families continued to return. Some retired here, giving the area a permanent cultural tradition that shows today in regular art and music events.

The land is beautiful and the mountains a little less craggy than the Presidential Range to the east. Towns here have less of a seasonal air about them, being year-round communities with their own economic base. Downtown stores cater more to local needs than to tour-bus shopping expeditions. Hospitality is warm, and visitors return to the same inn year after year.

Country stores, covered bridges, farms, and mountain streams punctuate the miles of forests bordering the winding country roads. Only the stone walls that wind through the woodlands remind us that much of this land was once cleared for farming. It is a place for relaxing, exploring, and savoring.

Two Notches

The White Mountain National Forest's westernmost segment begins just south of Sugar Hill and Franconia. Route 116 continues past the Frost Place to the town of Easton, high in the hills and completely surrounded by the national forest. South of Easton on Route 112 is a wild and beautiful notch almost completely overshadowed by the fame of neighboring Franconia Notch.

The road through **Kinsman Notch** winds and curves and climbs until it reaches tiny Beaver Lake, a high mountain tarn, rockbound and icy cold. In its center rises a rocky, pine-clad island. The landscape here is wild and almost desolate under the slope of Mount Blue—but nowhere near as forbidding as it must have looked to Asa Kinsman and his wife. With their household goods on a two-wheeled cart pulled by oxen, they discovered that they had taken the wrong track to their new home in Landaff. Instead of turning back to go around the mountains that lay in their way, they hacked a path through the notch. If you take a turn you didn't plan on or miss the road you wanted, just remember the Kinsmans and take heart.

At its top the notch opens out, giving excellent views down the valley to the east. The narrowness and curves of the road at the top give a real sense of this being a pass, more so than some of the better-known notches. (You may notice that the state highway map has the Kinsman Notch label a little to the east of its actual location 6 miles from North Woodstock.)

Franconia Notch is one of the most frequently visited spots in New Hampshire, and it is the home of the state's symbol, The Old Man of the Mountains. It was to protect the fragile ledges of this famous stone profile from the dangers of blasting that Interstate 93 was stopped just below the notch and resumed just above it. It took a U.S. congressman with the courage to dig in his heels and take on the whole of Washington, but the integrity of the notch was saved, and its hidden treasures remain in seclusion despite the number of visitors at its famous attractions. A bicycle path runs the length of the notch, crossing the highway through specially built underpasses.

A trail from the glacial formation known as the Basin leads to **Cascade Brook and Kinsman Falls.** Although these cascades are not ten minutes' level walk from the Basin, they are never crowded and provide a fine place to picnic or just explore. The ledges over which the brook slides and drops have been worn into graceful curves, potholes, tiny flumes, and gorges by the brook. In places the water spreads over the granite in a smooth sheet; elsewhere it falls in ribbons from pool to pool. You can climb through the woods along the trail or up the sloping face of the ledges. When water is high or the weather rainy, it's better to stay on the trail and avoid the slippery rocks. But on a nice day, with the sun warming both the rocks and the water, kids could spend all day here exploring the "caves" formed by tumbled boulders beside the falls and sliding from pool to pool through the water shoots. There are even whirlpool "baths" where you can cool off fast and see clearly how potholes are formed. Make sure, however, that the current is not too strong before you jump in.

Above, via the trail, you will find Kinsman Falls. There is no sign and you will have to take a steep side trail down to the left to reach the falls. While this waterfall of about 20 feet, shooting out from a flume, is impressive, the cascades below invite you to spend more time. They are a participatory, not a spectator, sport.

At the head of the notch, by the base of the Aerial Tramway, is the **New England Ski Museum.** Permanent and changing exhibits tell the story of this sport with historical equipment, photographs, art, and even changing fashions in skiwear. Open daily December 27 to March 31, 11:00 A.M. to 4:00 P.M., and May 20 to October 15, 11:00 A.M. to 5:00 P.M., the admission is only $1.00. Write The New England Ski Museum, P.O. Box 267, Franconia 03580; call (603) 823-7177.

The Aerial Tramway is well worth the trip. This was the first aerial mountain tramway in the United States and was considered a remarkable feat of engineering for the 1930s. The original tramway was replaced in 1980 by the present eighty-passenger cars that make the ascent to the summit in five minutes. One of the original cars is part of the ski museum. In the winter, the tramway is a ski lift for Cannon Mountain Ski Area and runs daily as long as there is snow for skiing. From late May to early October it runs daily from 9:00 A.M. to 4:30 P.M. (603-823-5563). The ride costs $7.00.

The Rim Trail can be reached from the top of the aerial tramway or via the Kinsman Ridge trail from the head of Franconia Notch. It offers hikers panoramic views into the notch and across the Franconia and Presidential ranges along the exposed rim and from the observation tower at the end. Notice the scar on the steep facing slope of Mount Lafayette, caused by a 1959 landslide that covered the road through the notch with 27 feet of debris. Even today, the physical forces of weathering and erosion continue the work of the glaciers in changing the landscape of the notches. Be sure to watch for peregrine falcons that nest on Eagle Cliff, below, where golden eagles once nested.

North of the Notches

Over the hills, on Route 117, lies Sugar Hill, stretched along the top of a ridge overlooking some of the White Mountains' most beautiful scenery. It's the kind of genteel town where people wave to you from their front porches as you go for an evening walk. **Harman's Store** should be your first stop, for fine aged cheddar that bears no resemblance to the grocery-store stuff. Harman's sends cheese and first-run New Hampshire maple syrup to people all over the country who don't really believe that there is a town named Sugar Hill. The secret of their cheese is that they buy fine aged cheddar and then age it themselves for two more years. You'll find fine New Hampshire jams and jellies, soldier beans, common crackers, and whole wheat pancake flour here, too, and all grades of the New Hampshire maple syrup that gave Sugar Hill its name. They also sell Vermont syrup for those people who won't believe that maple trees grow all over New England, New York, and Quebec (but they snicker a little behind their counter when they do). Open year-round, daily May to October, closed Sundays November to April. Call Harman's Cheese and Country Store at (603) 823–8000.

Across the street is the **Historical Museum.** Housed in two buildings, the exhibits show, through an exceptional collection of old photographs, artifacts, carriages, and furnishings, the daily life of early settlers and Sugar Hill's heyday as a summer resort. There is the kitchen from a stagecoach tavern with its original furnishings, a blacksmith shop, the ornate wagon of a local hotel, and even the guest books and menus. Admission is only $1.00 (50 cents for seniors). Open from July 1 through late October, Thursday and Saturday, 1:00 to 4:00 P.M., and Sunday, 2:00 to 5:00 P.M. (603–823–8142).

Within walking distance of both of these is **Hilltop Inn.** This is one of those places that friends hesitate to tell you about because they are afraid that it will become so popular that there won't be room for them. The 1895 Victorian home is decorated with period furniture but offers every modern comfort. Big beds, plenty of pillows for late-night readers, flannel sheets, and pieced quilts individually designed for each room are just a few of the luxuries. But the real charm of the Hilltop Inn is its owners, Meri and Mike Hern. Their offbeat sense of humor and irrepressible enthusiasm make old friends out of strangers from the first rumble of Mike's contagious chuckle. Guests raved about Meri's breakfasts for so long that they have finally opened for dinner as well. Local residents who've been guests at their home may keep the dining room full, so be sure to make dinner reservations. Open all year; children (even babies) and pets welcome. Write The Hilltop Inn, Main Street, Sugar Hill 03585; call (603) 823–5695.

There is a real sense of community about Sugar Hill and even short-term guests quickly become part of it. Local residents have built benches in front of the church so people can watch the sunset in comfort, and the whole town turns out in May for the

Hilltop Inn, Sugar Hill

annual luncheon and sale by the Willing Workers, a local ladies volunteer society. Since its heyday as a summer resort, Sugar Hill has had a flourishing arts community and hosts the **North Country Chamber Players** annual summer festival in the Meeting House on Friday evenings in July and August. Members of this organization hold first-chair positions in major orchestras. For a complete schedule of concerts write Box 99, Franconia 03580 or call (603) 869-3154.

For a view of the town and valley, as well as a view of the private world of Sugar Hill's grand past, drive or walk down the maple-lined Lover's Lane and go left on Grand View Road. It is at its best in the late afternoon as the sun lights the facing hillside crowned with the white houses of Main Street. The estates on either side of the road are impressive, and you can turn around where the pavement ends at Maplehurst Farm.

In the valley of the Gale River, east of Sugar Hill, is the town of Franconia. Right in the center of town is the small wooden building of **The Franconia Marketplace.** This houses a quartet of shops well worth visiting. At the back is the factory store of Gale River Cottons, with bargains on over one hundred styles of fine cotton dresses and other clothing. This Franconia company supplies its 100% cotton clothing to some of the finest catalog houses (603–823–8835). Next door is the Tiffany Workshop, studio of a family of stained-glass artists. Along with lampshades, they have smaller items and handmade jewelry. They also repair stained glass and will do custom work (603–823–5539).

The Grateful Bread bakes organic whole-grain bread seven days a week in the summer. Along with breads, they bake whole wheat muffins, cookies, granola, and other goodies. Stop in on Wednesday or Friday for their sourdough French bread (603-823-5228). In the front, with tables overlooking Main Street, is the Cannonball Cafe and Deli. If you are planning a hike to Zealand Falls or a day's drive in the mountains, stop here first for a picnic lunch. Better yet, order it ahead. Their classy lunches to go are so good that local hostesses order them regularly for their house guests. Lunches, espresso, and cappuccino are served daily 10:00 A.M. to 6:00 P.M. from June through September, and dinner is served from 5:00 to 9:00 P.M. Thursday, Friday, and Saturday evenings. The menu is filled with international surprises, but there is always a curry on Thursdays (603–823–7478).

Just to the north, across from LaFayette Regional School, look for picnic tables along the river. Behind these, across the river, you will see the stone ruins of New Hampshire's only remaining stone iron furnace, a vestige of a thriving industry from 1811 to the 1850s. Ore was smelted here from the richest vein then known, only 3 miles away on a hillside in Sugar Hill.

South of the village, off Route 116, the **Robert Frost Place** is a small weathered farmhouse, its mailbox marked R. FROST. Along with Robert Frost memorabilia and autographed first editions, there is a slide show, a nature trail marked with lines of his poetry, and a rare collection of his less-known work: Christmas card verses. Open Saturday and Sunday 1:00 to 5:00 P.M. Memorial Day to Columbus Day and every afternoon except Tuesday in July and August. The Frost Place is in Franconia; call (603) 823–5510.

The Ammonoosuc

Bethlehem, now a quiet town stretched out along a ridge, was once a major resort capital of the White Mountains. Along its main street stood thirty of the biggest and the grandest hotels, a summer-long procession of splendor and gaiety. They are gone now, but the elegant cottages that surrounded them are still there, today serving as bed and breakfasts, and so is the pure pollen-free mountain air that attracted the first visitors.

Its quiet streets and airy location make Bethlehem a good base for exploring the national forest, where the ban on commercial activity leaves no lodging for those who don't enjoy camping. **The Mulburn Inn** is a bed and breakfast in the Ivie Estate built for the heiress of the Woolworth fortune. The woodwork of maple, mahogany, oak, and ash is in mint condition, and the guests are served afternoon tea in a round sitting room (even the window glass is curved) in front of an Italian tile fireplace. Rooms are beautifully furnished and unique—one has its original raspberry-pink art deco bathroom fixtures, and another has the town's only elevator for a closet. Surrounded by three acres of lawn and framed by maple trees, The Mulburn Inn is beautiful at any season and open year-round. Write the inn at Main Street, Bethlehem 03574; call (603) 869–3389.

There are, it is said, more architectural styles in Bethlehem than in any other New England town. It's easy to believe. But the most unusual must be **The Bells,** a pagoda-shaped, three-story cottage whose top floor is a single small room. The roof curves upward at each corner, with bells suspended there from curved dragon tails. This flight of Victorian fancy was built by a Methodist minister who had never seen the Orient except in his imagination. It is now a very unusual bed and breakfast, its three guest suites decorated in high Victorian style. The 1894 "Regina" music box in the parlor plays "I Can't Begin to Tell You," except at Christmas when it plays (need we tell you?) "O Little Town of Bethlehem." Open all year. Write The Bells, Strawberry Hill Street, P.O. Box 276, Bethlehem, 03574; call (603) 869–2647.

Both of these unique lodgings are within walking distance of **Rosa Flamingo's,** known for the best pizza in the mountains but offering a far more varied selection of lunches and dinners. Their "Crusty Loaf" of garlic bread topped with roast beef, ham, or salami and mozzarella cheese is plenty for two hungry people; the fruit medley is fresh and equally generous; and the mushrooms stuffed with seafood are scrumptious. Rosa Flamingo's is on Main Street in Bethlehem; call (603) 869–3111.

Also along Main Street is the outlet store for **Nanook Children's Wear.** You've seen them in boutiques and fashionable catalogs, but you've probably never seen them at these prices. Look for the $15 boxes, where you can pull out eyelet party dresses or whatever they have too many of that week. This is a good place to stock up for Christmas. Nanook Children's Wear is on Main Street in Bethlehem (603–869–5761).

The Rocks, west of Bethlehem on Route 302, a late nineteenth-century farm estate, is now in the care of the Society for the Protection of New Hampshire Forests. The double stone walls, the buttresses, and the lower story of the Victorian barn were built of stones cleared from the rolling pastures and meadows that surround the house and barns. A free leaflet describes the sights along a 2-mile self-guided trail past a highly original sawmill-pigpen, past a bee house, and through forest and wetlands. The terraced gardens and pool are not groomed to within an inch of their lives, but flowers bloom through the seasons in a state of benign neglect, with forget-me-nots, bluebells, delphinium, lilacs, roses, daffodils, violets, and water lilies.

Seasonal activities are planned on weekends year-round, with a Halloween festival, hay-wagon tours of the Christmas tree plantation (along with cut-your-own sales), a winter forest festival with logging demonstrations, snowshoe tours, maple sugaring, and a wildflower festival. Nature trails and gardens are free and always open; there are fees for special programs, and registration is necessary for some. Write Society for the Protection of New Hampshire Forests, The Rocks, RFD #1, Bethlehem 03574; call (603) 444–6228.

Off Prospect Street and also managed by the same society is the Bretzfelder Memorial Park, seventy-seven acres of forest, pond, mountain brook, and picnic area connected by walking and cross-country trails. A leaflet tells about the various trees and signs along the trails explain the natural history and ecology. The story of Mr. Bretzfelder and his favorite tree (the tree is still alive even after major surgery) is told on a sign by the entrance. On Wednesday evenings in July and August at 8:00 P.M., the Evening Rambles explore some aspect of the park—its nocturnal animals, wildflowers, or other subject. No admission is charged; call (603) 444–6228 for dates and a description of the programs.

113

Maplewood was not just the largest and grandest of the local hotels; it was a village of its own with Victorian railroad station, farms to provide food for its dining rooms, a sugar bush that yielded one hundred gallons of syrup each spring, a golf course, and a casino with a ballroom, movie theater, and full bowling alley. The hotel is gone, but the village of Maplewood is still on the map. The restored casino with its stone tower still guards the golf course and four wonderful old "cottages"—great hulking things with porches and gabled windows—are situated in a row just east of the casino.

Beyond them is a little shrine by the side of the road with a lovely story to tell. From the beginning of the century until 1949, underprivileged boys from a Boston industrial school were brought up in the summers to work as caddies at the Maplewood. In 1958, a number of the former caddies, many of them prominent and successful, built the shrine. To this day these men gather at Maplewood for a reunion each summer.

Not far from Bethlehem, on its way to Whitefield, Route 142 drops down a long steep hill. At the very bottom, just as the road curves to the left, is a weathered farm and an auto body shop. Right in the middle of this, with no sign, is the tiny brown workshop of a man who has been honored by the President and whose work is on permanent display at The Smithsonian Institution. **Newt Washburn** is a fourth-generation Abenaki basketmaker, one of fewer than half a dozen who have continued in this art. He has designed and made his own tools, the knives and splitters with which he turns an ash log into a finely woven basket. On a full-sized basket each splint is the thickness of a growth ring separated from the log, but for smaller ones Newt splits each one in half to keep its thickness in proportion to the its width. If you've ever longed to own an original, museum-quality Abenaki basket, you'll find them in this tiny workshop—or displayed in front on the hood of an old car. Newt will show you the whole process, from log to basket, and his scrapbook too. Baskets run from $55.00 to $100.00, a real bargain for an original by a craftsman of his reputation. Newt Washburn's workshop is in Bethlehem Hollow (603–869–5894).

Arriving in Littleton on Route 302, **Bishop's Ice Cream Shoppe** is in a white house on the right. If you can think of any excuse to stop and try this ice cream, do it. You can sit at picnic tables on the lawn or inside the upbeat green and white ice cream parlor while you enjoy the old favorite flavors or one of their unique recipes. For calorie watchers or those with cholesterol problems, there are sorbets rich with the taste of real fruit, not the imitation candy-like flavorings. The Bishop's Bash is filled with chunks of brownie, walnuts, and chocolate chips, and their Brandy Alexander ice cream "is as close to the real thing that we serve at our New Year's Eve party as we can get without a liquor license," the owner explains. Light lunches are available, including a tempting spinach salad served in a waffle cone basket of whole wheat or spicy corn. Open daily until 9:00 P.M. from mid-April until mid-October at 78 Cottage Street in Littleton; call (603) 444–6039.

Throughout northern New Hampshire you will see photographs of the White Mountains "the way we were" during the Golden Age. Most of these were reproduced from stereoscopic view cards which, when seen through the double lenses of a special viewer, jumped into a three-dimensional landscape or scene. They were the forerunner of the Viewmaster and were a prime source of home entertainment. The major manufacturer of these cards was the Kilburn Brothers Stereoscopic View factory in Littleton.

In the bottom level of the Queen Anne-style Town Building (you can't miss its round, white, four-story tower) is the **Historical Museum.** It contains, along with other local artifacts, an exhibition on the Kilburn stereoscopic views. The museum is open Wednesdays from 1:30 to 4:30 P.M.; at other times call (603) 444–6586 for information.

Stamp or coin collectors will want to go a short distance past the Town Building on Route 116 as far as Union Street to visit the **Littleton Stamp and Coin Company.** For decades this company has provided collectors all over the world with both common and rare postage stamps; several generations of collectors began as children, receiving monthly packets of stamps "on approval" from Littleton, and still rely on their knowledge and integrity. You'll find them at 253 Union Street in Littleton; call (603) 444-5386.

If you have ever spent much time in the north country in February, you know a restaurant must be good if people are willing to stand in line on a winter day waiting to get in. But that is exactly what they do in order to eat Sunday brunch at **Tim-Ber Alley.** Their eclectic menu changes weekly and is constantly full of surprises inspired by cuisines from all over the world. They don't take reservations or credit cards, and they don't advertise. Evidently they don't have to. Open year-round for dinner and Sunday brunch in the alley behind 28 Main Street, Littleton; call (603) 444–6142.

Thayers Hotel is among the oldest of New Hampshire's inns, with a three-story Doric portico and a tall pediment. Three upper floors of attractive guest rooms are set along the wide sitting room hallways characteristic of its nineteenth-century origins. Guests will want to climb to its octagonal cupola for a view down into the whole town.

For a pleasant picnic spot, continue straight ahead at the west end of Main Street instead of following Route 302. You'll see The Dells on your left, with shaded picnic tables and fireplaces. You'll find it just before you come to I-93. There are herons and other birds around the pond, and the fishing area here is kept stocked and reserved for children up to age fifteen.

Avoid the interstate here by taking Route 18 to the Connecticut River, which forms both the Vermont border and a huge lake behind **Moore Station Dam.** One of the major power-generating dams in the northeast, it has a visitors' center where visitors are welcome to learn about the dam and to enjoy the adjacent picnic area and boat launch on the reservoir. Write the New England Power Company, North Monroe 03771 or call (603) 638–2327.

Route 135 plays hide-and-seek with the Connecticut River through valley farmland to Woodsville. You can either return to the Littleton area on Route 302 or take Route 112 from Bath to Franconia and Kinsman notches.

In Bath be sure to stop at **The Brick Store,** which has been open in the center of town since 1804. Without being "ye olde general store" about it, this emporium manages to retain the feel and much of the merchandise of an old country store while remaining a useful shopping place for local residents. Top shelves are lined with old tins, a thread cabinet, and other vintage store memorabilia, and the home-made fudge is displayed in a glass case. There's a wheel of cheddar on the counter and four shelves of buffalo-plaid wool shirts, a hot item here in the winter. Notice the slanted counter fronts which make room for hoop skirts. If you stop here for a sandwich (if you don't find one you like in the fridge they'll make one up for you), enjoy it sitting on the front porch with a view of Main Street and the old Mobil sign with the red Pegasus.

Behind the store is the **Bath Village Bridge,** a covered bridge so long that motorists are asked to turn on their headlights when entering it. Built in 1832 at a cost of $3,500, it still has its original arches. Be sure to notice its construction (all covered bridges are not built in the same way), a fine example of a Burr arch structure. At 400 feet, it is the longest in New Hampshire and one of the oldest still in use in America.

Bath has two other covered bridges, one of which is just off Route 112 in the village of Swiftwater. Farther along Route 112 and the Wild Ammonoosuc (don't let this confuse you—there are three different Ammonoosuc rivers in the area), where the road parallels the river for a stretch, there is a spot where hopeful prospectors have had moderate luck panning for gold. You may see their vehicles parked along the road. Route 112 leads to Kinsman Notch.

Northeast of Bath on Route 302 is **Upper Village,** a cluster of eight homes remarkable enough to make almost anyone ease up on the gas pedal. The most imposing are three grand brick mansions built in the early 1800s. Also set in the carefully manicured grounds, which cover both sides of the road, are other homes and huge, yellow clapboard barns with steep-pitched roofs, all in pristine condition. You expect to see a sign with the name of the museum, but these are private homes, and there are still members of the original family that built them living here, eleven generations later. Jeremiah Hutchinson, the first of them, moved to Bath in the winter of 1781 with his wife and twelve children. As you might imagine, it took two sleighs to bring them. There's no place to stop safely, and these are private homes, but this family village of extraordinarily well preserved Federal homes is unlike any other in the state.

Just south of Lisbon, on the south side of the road, is another historic group of homes, although of a much different sort. Early mills frequently provided housing for their workers, whose wages were often too low for them to afford adequate housing on their own. The company houses were built in rows, all alike, and called by such names as "Ten Commandments" or "Dirty Dozen." Most of the houses are long gone, but eleven of them stand here in their original row.

Lisbon offers another view of the state, one that you have glimpsed from the hardscrabble farms on the back roads. This is a town with lots of guts and little money, but every year it looks just a little bit more prosperous—another house freshly painted, another porch straightened. They have a Lilac Time Festival toward the end of every May. A real hometown event, it has pancake breakfasts, chicken barbecue, races, a golf tournament, quilt show, flea market, crafts, bands, singers, and a Saturday night dance. It's a time of year when summer attractions haven't opened and only the savvy traveler knows it to be a lovely and uncrowded season for a visit. For this year's dates and schedule, write the Lisbon Chamber of Commerce, Lisbon 03585 or call (603) 838-6336.

Off the Beaten Path in the North Country

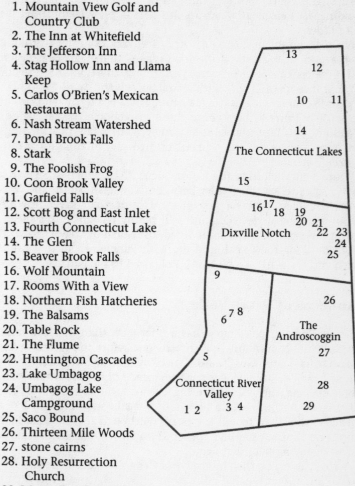

1. Mountain View Golf and Country Club
2. The Inn at Whitefield
3. The Jefferson Inn
4. Stag Hollow Inn and Llama Keep
5. Carlos O'Brien's Mexican Restaurant
6. Nash Stream Watershed
7. Pond Brook Falls
8. Stark
9. The Foolish Frog
10. Coon Brook Valley
11. Garfield Falls
12. Scott Bog and East Inlet
13. Fourth Connecticut Lake
14. The Glen
15. Beaver Brook Falls
16. Wolf Mountain
17. Rooms With a View
18. Northern Fish Hatcheries
19. The Balsams
20. Table Rock
21. The Flume
22. Huntington Cascades
23. Lake Umbagog
24. Umbagog Lake Campground
25. Saco Bound
26. Thirteen Mile Woods
27. stone cairns
28. Holy Resurrection Church
29. Moose Brook State Park

The North Country

The north country isn't for everyone. The nearest mall is hours away; if the local grocery store-cum-tackle and bait shop doesn't have it, you won't need it here.

Nightlife consists of swapping fishing or birding adventures in front of the fire or soothing muscles tired from canoeing, hiking, or skiing. If there is a Jacuzzi in this part of New Hampshire, it's well hidden.

But if the sight of a moose with a full rack of antlers drinking from a pool at the side of the road makes your heart beat faster, and if the cry of a loon is your favorite song, this is your Serengeti.

You'll meet people here with character, not the "ayuh" and hay-seed-style characters, but the real stuff. There is a ready wit born of the sense of humor necessary to those who choose the backwoods as a home. It's tent and canoe country, with a few fine lodgings for those who prefer their adventures to end in time for a full-course dinner.

Route 3 stays close to the Connecticut River, which at Stewartstown ceases to be the border between New Hampshire and Vermont. Travelers who have seen the Connecticut River flowing through southern New England will hardly recognize this meandering little brook as the same river. Just north of Stewartstown is a sign marking the crossing of the 45th Parallel. From that point north you are closer to the North Pole than to the equator.

Connecticut River Valley

No New England golf course has a finer view than the panorama of the White Mountains that spreads out before the greens at the **Mountain View Golf and Country Club.** Overlooking the course from the other side is the vast facade of the Mountain View Hotel, among the last of the big White Mountain resorts. The hotel is empty now, and a little sad, but still standing tall, like a dowager who's had to sell her pearls. Although the building is in serious need of work, some upkeep is underway, and there is hope that she may reopen once again.

Across the street, the clubhouse of the golf course is freshly renovated and serves lunches daily from 11:00 A.M. to 4:00 P.M. A paneled dining room overlooks the course, and the terrace overlooks the swimming pool. Daily and weekly memberships are offered for the pool, golf course, and tennis courts. Open from May through foliage season, on Mountain View Road in Whitefield; call (603) 837–3885.

For a fine dinner in the Jefferson-Whitefield area, don't miss **The Inn at Whitefield** on Route 3 just at the intersection with Mountain View Road. The atmosphere is elegant and upbeat, with a lively northern Italian cuisine. Pollo Forte Freddo is an outstanding appetizer of chilled roasted chicken with fresh vegetables and a tangy dipping sauce, too much as a first course for two. The chef is very accommodating, changing combinations, pasta varieties, and accompaniments as requested, and the service has the enthusiasm usually only seen at a family-run inn. Every evening brings new specials, such as tuna steak with roasted red bell peppers. The sauces are light, the baguettes hot, and the table flowers fresh. It is open year-round serving dinner only. For reservations call (603) 837–2760.

A short distance away on Route 116 is Jefferson, an unadorned town set along a ridge facing the mountains. Only the outbuildings remain of the Waumbek Hotel, which once dominated its crossroads, but there are still delightful accommodations in town at **The Jefferson Inn.** To the original 1896 Victorian house with its tower and wraparound porch, young owners Greg Brown and Bertie Koelewijn have added a new ell. Finding woodworking and other architectural detail to either match or fit the style of the original house, they have given the new rooms the same grace as the older ones.

Quilts warm most of the beds, and antiques are mixed with more recent furnishings, creating a nice balance of comfort and style. Families with well-behaved children will enjoy the corner suite on the first floor, the Green Room with its rounded tower corner and huge Victorian bed adjoined by a smaller room with a brass bed and a high-ceilinged bath with a claw-footed tub.

The breakfast room is bright, with a view up across the back meadow. It has a charming assortment of antique and hand-crafted table accessories. One table has a silver-topped nineteenth-century sugar bowl with sugar tongs built right into the lid, and another, a cut-crystal maple syrup pitcher. Tea is served in a full-sized old teapot encased in an embroidered tea cozy. Along with a main course and sausage or bacon comes a freshly baked breakfast bread or perhaps a big square pan of baked apple pancake (more like a coffee cake) fresh from the oven. Too much? Your hosts will wrap the leftovers for you to carry on with you (it's great cold as a snack on the road). Reasonably priced, the inn is open all year except for April and November. Write The Jefferson Inn, Route 2, Jefferson 03583 or call (603) 586–7998.

Just east of the inn on the north side of the road stands a group of "cottages" of the same era. Of wood and stone, each shows the unmistakable marks of the late 1800s. All along Route 2 to Jefferson Highlands there are cottages of wealthy former summer residents, some nearly hidden by foliage.

If you are tired of carrying your camera bags and your bird and wildflower guides on your explorations into the national forest, go to **Stag Hollow Inn and Llama Keep.** They provide llamas that will carry packs on half- or full-day treks on White Mountain trails. Or, if you would just like to admire these gentle creatures from a comfortable distance, visit the keep and spend a night in the tastefully restored farmhouse. The trek destinations are seldom-traveled trails tailored to your own interests, such as local history (complete with ghost villages and cellar holes) or woodland flora. The inn is open year-round except for mid-April to mid-May, with treks May through October. Write Stag Hollow Inn, R.F.D. 1, Jefferson 03583; call (603) 586–4598 (preferably after 5 P.M.).

Close by is the northern end of the road over Jefferson Notch (see p. 103), in case you decide to travel it from this direction. The road is well marked from the Jefferson end.

Lancaster's main street still has the prosperous look of the late nineteenth century, with brick buildings and small storefronts lining both sides. Some very fine Victorian homes and a distinctive courthouse coexist with newer structures on the north end of town. Look for the monument in Centennial Park on the left: An exquisite bronze fox stands there atop a small granite boulder.

If hunger overtakes you here try **Carlos O'Brien's Mexican Restaurant**, just off the main street behind the Lancaster National Bank. It's now owned by Italians, but they still serve good flautas, enchiladas, and the usual Mexican offerings at modest prices. Paisano blood runs deep, though, and on Wednesday nights they serve Italian specialties. The restaurant is at 12 Middle Street in Lancaster (603–788–2072).

Farther north on Route 3, just before you get to Groveton, Route 110 branches to the right (east) and travels along the upper

Ammonoosuc River. To the north lies the **Nash Stream Watershed,** an area whose future has been the subject of an intense battle among land developers, the state, and several conservation groups. Forty thousand acres of it have finally been secured as public lands, a mixed habitat for hawks, falcons, and smaller birds in a forested valley. Access is via Emerson Road, about 2 miles east of Groveton. Follow it another 2 miles to a fork, and then go left. After about 4.5 miles of dirt road, a right fork leads uphill to Little Pond Bog, a fine spot for fly fishing high above the valley. In the winter this area is crisscrossed by cross-country ski trails.

If you continue straight ahead less than half a mile instead of taking the right, you come to **Pond Brook Falls,** a series of waterfalls known to very few people outside of Groveton and Stark. Just after crossing a culvert you will see a pull-out area to the right. Park there and follow the trail a short distance to the lower falls (watch for moose tracks—this is a favorite path for them, too). You'll hear the falls before you see them, and then you'll see only part of them. Continuing up hill, the path ends at a second falls; from here the best route is over the sloping granite ledge alongside the rushing water. Except during spring runoff, there is plenty of room on this 50-foot-wide span of rock for both you and the brook.

Keep going upstream for an ever-changing series of falls, some gushing through narrow chutes and others spread in a filmy veil across a wide ledge. As you reach the top of each, you look up to see another of different size and shape. It's New Hampshire's sampler of waterfall styles. Do be careful after a rain or in the early spring when the rocks are wet, since they can be quite slippery to climb. On wet days, go through the woods next to the falls where the footing is more secure.

Back on Route 110, continue on to visit **Stark,** an idyllic mountain town clustered around its covered bridge under Devil's Slide, a 700-foot precipice. During World War II, Stark housed a camp for German prisoners of war. The remarkable story of how these men, taken prisoner in North Africa, became friends of local farmers during their long winters together is told in *Stark Decency* by Allen Koop. (See book list, p. 138)

Rock hounds take note: At Diamond Ledge on Long Mountain and also on the south slope of Percy Peak, about 200 feet below the summit, amethyst is found in the surface rock; topaz is found at Diamond Ledge. You will need to get thorough directions locally or use a topographic map.

Each June, dozens of fiddlers gather in Stark for the Old Time Fiddlers Contest at Whitcomb Field. Bring the whole family, lawn chairs, and a picnic lunch or buy your lunch there. Admission is charged. Call (603) 636–1325 for dates and details.

Groveton is a paper mill town, although the enormous piles of pulpwood, the logjams in the river, and the terrible smell that once characterized it are long gone. There is a covered bridge, painted white, and a vintage logging steam locomotive near its main intersection. McKenzie's Diner on Route 3 just north of town serves generous portions, homemade fries, and good breakfasts. If you are lucky, you will see the pair of large raccoons that the staff has befriended poking about outside the kitchen door.

Between the towns of Stratford and North Stratford, on the right, look for **The Foolish Frog.** This unexpected roadside museum is the personal twenty-five-year collection of Carol Hawley and houses hundreds upon hundreds of frogs made of every conceivable material and in every imaginable style. Along with frog whatsits and gimcracks there are fine folk art sculptures including an Indonesian frog deity, a frog flute from Colombia, a rubber frog from the Amazon, plus pottery, baskets, puzzles, bottle stoppers, batiks, mechanical banks, puppets, and potholders. It is fascinating to see how a creature common throughout the world has been adapted as a design motif in so many ways. A small shelf in the center of the room displays frogs for sale, including several unique wooden toys designed and made by Carol and her husband. There is no admission charge, but there is a discreet little box for donations, which help to keep the collection growing. The Foolish Frog is open from May through foliage season, but there are no set hours. Write RR#1, Box 428, Route 3, North Stratford 03590 or call (603) 636–1887.

The Connecticut Lakes

The town of Pittsburg is geographically the largest in New Hampshire, over 20 miles wide and covering more than 360 square miles. The entire tip of New Hampshire, from the Maine to Vermont borders to the international border with Canada, lies within its boundaries. The whole town was an independent nation for three years beginning in 1832. Claimed by both New Hampshire and Canada, and with no decisive action taken by either to settle the issue, the Indian Stream Territory was left in chronic limbo. Tiring of this, and not wishing to be governed by either contender, the citizens voted their independence at a town meeting. This finally brought them to everyone's attention. After three years and a few altercations among the local militia, a Canadian sheriff's posse, and a small company of New Hampshire militia, the Republic of Indian Stream became the town of Pittsburg.

Within Pittsburg's borders lie all four of the Connecticut Lakes and Lake Francis, and mile after mile of forests, mountain streams, bogs, and assorted wilderness lands. Pittsburg's main (almost its only) road borders each lake in turn until it finally climbs the "height-of-land" to the Canadian border station. ("Height-of-land" is a term commonly used in the north country to describe the high point of any of the area's many ridges.) At nearly any point you may see deer or moose by the roadside.

What is unique here is the series of pristine water bodies. Uninhabited by man, these provide habitat for wild shorebirds found in few other places. Loon populations are increasing. You can put in a canoe on nearly any pond, and you are welcome to roam the woods roads built by the timber companies as long as they are not barred. The whole area abounds with trout.

Coon Brook Valley, a long, wide, marshy area cut by a woods road is a sure place to see moose at almost any time of day. To find it, look for a road marked MAGALLOWAY TOWER entering Route 3 from the right. Go a few yards north and take the road entering from the opposite side of Route 3. Just drive in and park in an open spot—you may even see moose before you park.

For an adventure into the outer reaches of the wilderness, but one that requires only a short hike, search out **Garfield Falls.** Take the above-mentioned gravel road marked MAGALLOWAY TOWER, following the tower signs until you reach the height of land (the top of the ridge). At this point a dirt road to the tower goes off to the right, but you should keep going. About 2 miles after you pass Paradise Camp on your left, you will go down a hill and see a road bearing off to the right (the road straight ahead of you may be blocked just below this). Follow the road to the right 1.1 mile to where it makes a sharp left turn and crosses a bridge. Take the dirt road right at the turn.

Coon Brook Valley, Pittsburg

It's narrow, but unless there have been heavy rains, it is easily passable without four-wheel drive. In another 1.1 mile the road opens out into a yard (an open area where logs are stored). Park there and look for a trail into the woods on the left side of the road. It may take a few minutes to find it if there have been logging operations there recently, but it is just to the right of a tree with several small forest signs on it, close by a tumble of large rocks.

Garfield Falls is only a five-minute walk from here, through a forest carpeted in the spring with trillium, clintonia, bunchberry, wood sorrel, and occasional moose droppings that look like piles of nutmegs beside (or in) the trail. The falls will be to your left, dropping off the facing side of a chasm into a pool almost directly under your feet. It comes through a zigzag shoot and then bounces off the boulder with such force that it has worn a depression in the face of the cliff as well as a cave at its base where its velocity creates a whirlpool. Below the falls the river is split by a giant boulder from which you can get an excellent view of the falls—and the deeply undercut bank that you were just standing on!

This is not a trip to begin with bald tires, with a near-empty gas tank, or in a downpour of rain, but it is quite an easy one. The distances aren't great, just slow to cover. Before you curse the timber companies for their cutting throughout this area, remember two points. First, you are traveling on their roads, which are the only access to these areas in case of forest fires. Second, their cutting, done with the techniques that they now employ, creates a far more inviting habitat for birds and animals than dense forest provides.

A little farther up Route 3, just above the Second Connecticut Lake, another timber road to the right leads to **Scott Bog and East Inlet.** The road curves down into a valley and across a stream to a rough T, where you should go left to find Scott Bog or right to find East Inlet. The latter is a former log drive impoundment from which logs were floated out on the spring thaw. In 1987, Champion Paper Company donated 426 acres of pristine pond and moose pasture here, including a tract of virgin spruce and fir, to the Nature Conservancy. The Scott Bog-East Inlet area is considered by birders to offer the best sightings in the north country, with spruce grouse, Canada jay, sixteen warbler varieties, and the rare black-backed woodpecker. Sighting of eighty to ninety species in three days is quite common here.

Wandering around on these woods roads is a lot easier and less nerve-wracking with the inexpensive map "Roads and Trails, Connecticut Lake Region" printed on waterproof paper and available at most stores in the area. Wherever you go you will find wilderness, with only an occasional birder, fisherman, or logging truck to share it with.

The Connecticut River, barely a trickle now, crosses the road above the Second Connecticut Lake, and the tiny Deer Mountain Campground sits on its northern banks. Its twenty campsites are rustic: no hot showers, flush toilets, or camp store here, but there is plenty of quiet and it is alive with birds. The Moose Falls Flowage, just north of the campground, is a good place to put in a canoe. The campground is open from May until the end of October.

Third Connecticut Lake has a boat ramp right off Route 3, but **Fourth Connecticut Lake** takes a bit more effort. Only about an acre in size, it is reached by a trail from the U.S. Customs station at the Canadian border. The trail, which is actually the cleared swath along the border, is "steep and rugged," as the map warns. Because it is rocky, it is not a hike for street shoes. Park and sign in at the customs station, where they will give you a trail map. It is only about a half mile to the seventy-five-acre site that Champion Paper Company donated to the Nature Conservancy in 1990. Be sure to walk around the upper part of the lake to find the spot where the first few drops of the mighty Connecticut River trickle from the rocks.

The Canadian border is so close and the view is so different from the other side that you should cross the border for a look. (If you are *not* a U.S. citizen you will need your documents.) Just over the ridge that forms the boundary, the land drops away into a broad flat valley filled with cleared farmland.

Magnetic Hill, a mystifying phenomenon that makes your car roll uphill, is just at the foot of the hill. There is usually a sign to mark the spot. Pull off to the side of the road, shift into neutral, take your foot off the brake, and see what happens.

Back in New Hampshire again you have no choice but to retrace your path down Route 3; it's the only road between the border and the center of Pittsburg. But there will be new deer and moose along the way and a different set of lake views.

The best way to enjoy this area is to settle in for a few days, and the best place to do that is in a comfortable log cabin or lodge overlooking a lake. **The Glen,** a former private estate, looks as though it had grown there with the tall spruce trees that line the shores of First Connecticut Lake. The big lodge is a convivial place with a huge stone fireplace and comfortable Adirondack log and maple furniture. There are rooms upstairs, or you can opt for the seclusion of your own cabin.

If you arrive on a cool evening in the spring or in the fall, there will be a roaring fire in your fireplace to warm your hands over. The atmosphere is comfortable, not cute. There are no frilly curtains or designer sheets, but you won't be roughing it either.

All meals are included in the rate, and they'll pack you a box lunch with a sandwich (seven kinds to choose from), fruit, cheese, dessert, candy bars, and drinks; they will even fill your thermos with hot coffee when you leave for your day's adventure. Dinners in the dining room are generous, including such entrees as haddock filet with shrimps and scallops, served with vegetables, pilaf, wine, and big bowls of ice cream for dessert. The whipped cream on your chocolate cream pie is real, and the vegetables in the salad bar are crisp and fresh. Breakfasts are hearty as well, and meals prepared to suit special diets are treated with the same careful attention as the main offerings.

The tone and warmth of The Glen is set by its owner, Betty Falton. She helps guests choose places to hike, fish, bird, or just wander around, suggesting routes and telling about her own favorite nooks and crannies. Boats are available for rent (she keeps them moored on various lakes so you won't have to haul them around), or you can bring your own. Betty loves her "neighborhood" and does everything that she can to help her guests enjoy it, but she stresses that this is not the place for everyone's taste. "If you can't walk to the brook without seeing something interesting, you don't belong here," she is quick to tell prospective guests when they call.

When the full moon rises over Mount Magalloway, reflecting in the lake and outlining the spiky silhouettes of the fir trees around the lake, it looks like the stage set for *Rose Marie*. If the lure of the wilderness charms you, there's no finer place to enjoy it. The Glen is open from mid-May to October, when you can call for reservations at (603) 538–6500. From December to April call Betty at (508) 475–0559, or call (800) 445–GLEN.

While the Glen serves meals to non-guests by reservation, you can also get a good breakfast, lunch, or dinner at the Midtown Restaurant. It may look a little tired on the outside, but this family-run restaurant serves well-prepared meals. Fries are homemade, sandwiches generous, and the clamroll overflows with whole clams. When you ask for a glass of milk here, it comes ice cold and in a sixteen-ounce tumbler. Open every day except Wednesday, all year-round.

South of Pittsburg you have a choice of roads. Route 145 covers the same route, but in a straighter line. At least on the map it's straighter—if you ironed out the hills, the length would probably be the same. The view from the hilltops, past hillside farms and forests to the skyline of mountains to the south, makes it a nice change from Route 3's river-bottom route.

Beaver Brook Falls drops almost onto Route 145, about 2½ miles before you reach Colebrook. You will see small parking areas on both sides of the road before you see the falls. Be prepared for a surprise, especially if it has rained recently—somehow one doesn't expect a waterfall this large to appear out of the woods, particularly on the side of the road. The top 35 feet of the falls are a straight drop, even more spectacular when rains or spring runoff have increased the flow of water so it spreads across the entire face of the cliff. Below, a series of cascades spill from pool to pool. At the foot of the falls is a small park with picnic tables and a swimming hole. If you aren't going into the tip of the state, you can get to the falls via Route 145 out of Colebrook (the sign is marked CLARKSVILLE), making the 5-mile side trip before going on to Dixville Notch.

Dixville Notch

Unlike most of New Hampshire's other notches, which run north and south, Dixville lies east and west. Route 26 follows the Mohawk River all the way from Colebrook to the notch itself, but before reaching Dixville there are a few side trips worth taking.

About 3 miles outside of Colebrook, look for East Colebrook Road going up the hill to your left. The road continues upward giving fine views over the notch. On your left, watch for a weathered house with a sign that says **WOLF MOUNTAIN.** Stop here for a fascinating short tour of a wolf-breeding farm. Dyanne Hodge raises wolf cubs, breeding them with Labs and Siberian Huskies to produce hybrids of 50% to 90% wolf.

This is not a fancy place; Dyanne does her share of running the family dairy farm and a mega-garden as well. But her enthusiasm for these wolf cubs is infectious. She sells the cubs to carefully selected owners—wolves bond for life—so ownership is not something to be undertaken at a whim. To be sure Dyanne will be there, or to inquire about cubs, call (603) 237–4116.

A little farther along, this road comes to an intersection at an old schoolhouse. A left will bring you to a unique lodging, **Rooms With a View.** Unlike most New Hampshire bed and breakfasts, this one is in a newly built home, set in a hilltop meadow with its porch rockers overlooking the Connecticut valley and Dixville Notch. The kitchen is in the center of the house, and you are welcome to watch Sonja bake her bread (fresh everyday and sweetened with their own honey) in the huge Tulikivi soapstone stove that dominates the room. Or you can just sit in the bright dining room and enjoy the view while she serves you a full, made-from-scratch country breakfast.

Each room is different, with a graceful mix of antique and new furniture. Beds are warmed by quilts pieced by Sonja, and each bathroom has a fuzzy, thick sheepskin mat. The house was built to share, and it's a warm and welcoming place to come home to after your north country travels. Open year-round. Write Rooms With a View, Forbes Road, Colebrook, 03576 or call (603) 237–5106.

Back on Route 26 look for Fish Hatchery Road, also on the left, and then for the almost immediate driveway to **Northern Fish Hatcheries.** Using the existing facilities of a recently closed state fish hatchery, Northern offers a beautiful, grassy-shored pool where you can practice your fly casting or learn from the beginning without a New Hampshire fishing license. Bring your own equipment or borrow their rods and reels. They'll show you how, and you pay by the inch for the fish that you catch. If you just want to practice fly casting, you can use barbless hooks, return your catch, and pay by the hour. The rainbow, brown, and brook trout range from 6 inches to 20 inches. There is also a show pond where you can see the fish. It's a good place for kids to learn to fish, and they are sure to enjoy visiting the rearing pools as well. The telephone number is (603) 237–4459.

For many visitors, the goal and the reward of the long trip to this far-off tip of the state is staying at the world-class grand hotel set just below the head of the notch. **The Balsams** is unique in so many ways that we'll mention only a few. Once one of many large resort hotels where city families came to spend the summer before the days of air conditioning, The Balsams is, if not the only one still open, at least the only one still thriving. One by one, these grande dames of the late nineteenth century have fallen on hard times, teetering between bankruptcy, reorganization, red ink, and the final closing of their doors. Alone, The Balsams has weathered the tough financial climates as well as it has weathered its natural climate. It has turned the harsh winters to advantage by opening a family ski area and miles of cross-country ski trails, keeping Lake Gloriette open for skating, giving snowshoe lessons, and offering the free use of snowshoes and cross-country skis.

Their success is even more surprising because of the hotel's remote location, but therein lies another unique feature. Unlike the other big hotels that were built in the busy White Mountain circuit, The Balsams stands alone, with none of the tourist attractions of the more heavily traveled routes. It is a gracious and highly civilized oasis in a vast wilderness, and its owners have turned that fact to their advantage. They have provided so many activities, sporting opportunities, social events, and gastronomic pleasures that it would take a week to enjoy them all. In the summer, there are golf, hiking, walks with a local naturalist, fishing (with or without a license) in the lakes and streams, boating, canoeing, tennis, moose watching, swimming, dancing (ballroom or disco), movies, cooking lessons, a daily sports program, and the opportunity just to sit on the wide veranda and look at the mountains.

One of the few resorts operating on the American plan, The Balsams includes all meals in the room rate, and you won't want to miss one. Breakfast is worth getting up for, no matter how late you danced in the ballroom the previous night. Lunch is a buffet of dishes including poached salmon, roast beef, lobster Newburg (all shellfish, no fillers), a salad of smoked duck with wild rice, sliced tongue, imported salamis, chilled and hot soups, breads and rolls from their own bakery, and an entire table of mouth-watering desserts, of which you are welcome to sample as many as your appetite allows. Dinner is more formal, with a wide choice of entrees as elegant and innovative or as traditional as you like. This is not the usual hotel dining room fare, and this top-quality cuisine is one of the primary reasons for the success of the entire resort.

Did we mention that the leader of the dance band used to be with Glenn Miller. . . or that The Balsams welcomes families and provides special activities, ski programs, and babysitting so that parents can enjoy some time to themselves as well? While there, don't miss Tilly's Balloons, the factory store for the local industry, where you can choose from a rainbow assortment of balloons displayed in jars, as in a jelly bean store. Or the room where the residents of Dixville gather every four years at midnight to cast the nation's first ballots of the presidential election. Write The Balsams, Dixville Notch 03576; call (603) 255-3400 or (800) 255-0800 in New Hampshire or (800) 255-0600 elsewhere.

Between meals at The Balsams, explore the notch. You can vary your level of exercise, beginning with a walk around the Lake Gloriette walking trail, a 1.4-mile loop, with the hotel's "Natural History Handbook" as your guide. More energy is required for the climb up to **Table Rock,** especially if you take the rock-strewn trail that goes almost straight up from the notch. A more gentle ascent can be made by a trail beginning near the Wilderness Ski Area entrance road. Table Rock overlooks The Balsams, the lake, and the notch, but it's no place for an acrophobic.

If you want to know where to buy hand-tied flies, hire a good fishing guide, ask about the "lonesome loon" in the lake, find Mable Sims's fish pond, or rent a canoe, ask Ray Gorman, the chief concierge at The Balsams. He's an experienced outdoorsman and a native of the area, the perfect concierge for such a resort.

The Flume is on the other side of the notch, and on your way there you can appreciate how wild this notch is compared to Franconia, Pinkham, and even Crawford notches. It's a *real* notch where you go over a hump in the road, through a cleft in the cliffs, and down a steep, winding road squeezed between two tree-covered walls. The difference is geological: The surface rock here has been tilted on end so that its strata stand upright, causing the craggy eroded points of rock that give it such a wild aspect.

About a mile past the head of the notch look for a picnic area on the left. The geology changes back to granite here, as Flume Brook carves a gorge over 200 feet long with sides so straight it almost seems to have been built from cut blocks of stone. It is 40 feet deep in places, as the brook drops from pool to pool and finally over the edge of a ledge. Walk along the rim, and in the spring look for trillium and white and pink lady's slippers beside the trail. They are protected species, so enjoy them in place.

Just a few yards down Route 26, this time on the right, is the road to a second picnic area. **Huntington Cascades** is reached by a short path to the brook and then a short walk upstream. The falls continue above the one that you can see from the base, but there is no trail up the steep slope beside the falls, so most visitors simply enjoy the lower section as it rushes in its curving path over the rocks. If you do go exploring here, be careful and stay away from the edge, which has been undercut by the brook. In case you wondered, the little cemetery by the entrance to the parking area contains the remains of some of the area's earliest settlers.

The 5 miles of road between Huntington Cascades and the town of Errol is a prime stretch for moose viewing, so drive slowly and keep watch. You can't miss the Errol International Airport, whose building is so tiny that its long name has to be abbreviated to fit across its facade.

Each of the two roads leaving from the far end of Errol's main street will take you to the Maine border. Route 16, to the left, offers a pleasant drive along the upper Androscoggin and the Magalloway rivers. Route 26 leads to the southern shores of **Lake Umbagog** and one of the most beautiful and unusual campgrounds in all of New England.

Lake Umbagog is a wildlife sanctuary, with one of the nation's largest loon nesting areas. Bald eagles have also nested there for several years, raising chicks of their own and even a chick from an adopted egg from New York State. Other bird life and, of course, moose abound.

Umbagog Lake Campground is, like most of this north country, not for everyone. "We cater to canvas," says owner Jim Willard, by which he means that they will accommodate your RV if they have room, but the campground is really designed for tents. Along with sites overlooking the length of Umbagog's blue waters, the shady wooded sites and the handful of cottages, there are over thirty wilderness campsites on islands or shores of the lake without road access. The farthest of these is 11 miles from the campground; Jim will take you to your site by motorboat if you don't want to paddle all the way. You can bring your own rowboat or canoe, or rent theirs, for exploring the lake.

These sites are isolated, at least a half mile apart, some on islands. They are not for beginning campers, but for the woods wise and the water wise they offer real camping that is very hard to find. Open from Memorial Day to mid-September, you can reserve sites. Write Umbagog Lake Campground, P.O. Box 181, Errol 03579; call (603) 482–7795.

In Errol, **Saco Bound** rents canoes and kayaks, as well as operating a full transportation service so you can put in at one place and be picked up at a different location. In the summer they offer reasonably priced guided day trips complete with a barbecue lunch. They operate a whitewater canoe and kayak school at Errol, as well as a campground for their customers. Write Saco Bound, Box 119, Center Conway 03813; call (603) 447–2177 or 447–3801.

The Androscoggin

South of Errol on Route 16 begins a scenic stretch where the road and the Androscoggin River travel side by side through **Thirteen**

Mile Woods. The river is wide and for the most part gentle, and there are put-ins at several different points. If you have ever held a paddle, you will long to be on the water in this flat reach where the trees overhang the water. There is even a campground, the Mollidgewock, right on the river and designed primarily for canoeists. It is open from mid-May to December 1. Be sure to call them at (603) 482–3373 to reserve a site, since its half-mile frontage on calm water and rapids is a favorite teaching area for groups learning whitewater techniques.

Motorists will find good places for a riverside picnic, or to just sit and watch the river traffic go by. Below the Thirteen Mile Woods is another area frequented by moose, where it is not unusual to see them beside (or in) the road.

North of Berlin look for the **stone cairns** in the river, among the last reminders of the days of the logging drives that were common in this country during the nineteenth and early twentieth centuries. These mid-river cairns served as the point from which the great chain booms were secured. These captured and held a vast flotilla of logs during the annual spring release of the timber that had been harvested during the winter. As trees were cut during the winter, the logs were hauled into impoundment ponds. During the runoff, the dams holding these ponds were released. The water and logs in it broke into a wild frenzy of energy and wood that found its way downstream into the sawmills and paper plants of New England.

Berlin (pronounced with the accent on the first syllable) is a paper mill town; you can't miss the smokestacks of the James River Corporation. It has been a paper town ever since the first logging camp was established in 1825, although the first paper mill didn't open until 1852. At one time, it was estimated that the paper produced in Berlin annually would cover a road 15 feet wide that would run nineteen times around the world. The mill brought immigrants from Canada and as far away as Russia. These ethnic groups have mixed and moved, but a few traces remain from the days when church services in the community were conducted in five different languages.

Saint Anne's church, a classic French-Canadian brick structure, rises like a fortress in the center of town, enormously tall, with an oversized statue on top. But far more unexpected is **Holy Resurrection Church.** Take Mount Forist Street, which intersects with Main Street near the post office, and follow it up the hill. When

Russian Orthodox Church, Berlin

we say *up*, we mean almost straight up what may well be New Hampshire's steepest street. Just before the street ends, go left on Russian Street, still going uphill, and look to your right. Six polished, gold-leafed, onion-shaped domes crown a gem of a Russian Orthodox church on the corner of Petrograd Street. Each dome is surmounted by a double patriarchal gold cross; the rest of the church is white. It sits above the city overlooking the smokestacks and rows of company housing below, a poignant and rare reminder of the homesickness of the many peoples that were propelled into this strange and new land.

On Jimtown Road, just off of Route 5 west of Gorham, is a very pleasant campground at **Moose Brook State Park.** Its forty-six sites are well spaced in open forest, with a few at the edge of a field. An ingenious warming pool brings the icy-cold waters of Moose Brook up to a more suitable temperature before it flows into the swimming pool downstream. There is a picnic area near the swimming pool. Be sure to notice the architecture of the administration building, which is a classic of Civilian Conservation Corps (CCC) construction. The park is open from late May through Labor Day. It is not possible to reserve campsites, but you can call (603) 466–3860 for information.

A Note about our Less Appealing Wildlife

While May's lilacs are safe as the state's flower, there is talk every spring about changing the state bird from the purple finch (which we rarely see) to the mosquito or blackfly, which we see all too often. Unless you have allergies to their bites, these springtime insects are merely an annoyance. They don't carry malaria or yellow fever as their tropical relatives do, and slapping them is a source of moderate exercise.

But in the north country, especially in May and June, it is wise to be prepared for them. Long sleeves, long pants, and shirts with collars will protect you when these voracious creatures are at their worst—evenings and mornings and in the deep woods.

Everyone has a favorite brand of repellent; we favor Natrapel for most places and Bens 100 for the worst conditions. Natrapel is the only repellent that we know of with EPA approval and which comes in a nonaerosol spray and a recyclable bottle. Both are New Hampshire products, created by people who know mosquitos intimately. For sources call (800) 258–4696 or write Tender Corp. P.O. Box 290, Littleton 03561.

Book List

Koop, Allen. *Stark Decency*. University Press of New England, 1988.

Milne, Lorus and Margery. *A World Alive*. Yankee Books, 1991.

Pike, Robert. *Tall Trees, Tough Men*. W. W. Norton and Company, 1967.

Thaxter, Celia. *An Island Garden*. Houghton Mifflin, 1988.

Yates, Elizabeth. *The Road Through Sandwich Notch*. Society for the Protection of New Hampshire Forests, 1973.

INDEX

Index

Index

Index

About the Authors

Barbara Radcliffe Rogers and Stillman Rogers have, jointly and singly, written and illustrated over 20 books, most of them on travel, wildlife, and gardening. Titles include *Galapagos*, *Safari*, *The Portugal Traveler*, *Big Cats*, and *Giant Pandas*. They have written and illustrated several books in the *Children of the World* series describing the lives and cultures of children from Agentina to Zambia. Barbara has written articles for *Yankee Magazine*, *Country Journal*, *Animal Kingdom*, *The Los Angeles Times*, and others including a column, "The Travel Advisor" for *The Walpole Gazette* in Walpole, New Hampshire. Stillman's photographs have illustrated these and other articles.

In *New Hampshire: Off The Beaten Path*, they write for the first time about their home state. Although they have explored its trails and back roads since childhood, they still find it as fascinating as the most exotic locales in their wide repertoire of travels.

UNITED STATES TRAVEL

Off the Beaten Path Series

These are the fine guides from our
Off the Beaten Path series designed for the traveler who
enjoys the special and unusual. Each book is by an author
who knows the state well, did extensive research, and per-
sonally visited many of the places, often more than once.
Please check your local bookstore for fine
Globe Pequot Press titles, which include:

To order any of these titles with MASTERCARD or VISA,
call toll-free (800) 243–0495; in Connecticut call
(800) 962–0973. Free shipping for orders of three or more
books. Shipping charge of $3.00 per book for one or two
books ordered. Connecticut residents add sales tax. Ask for
your free catalogue of Globe Pequot's quality books on
recreation, travel, nature, gardening, cooking, crafts, and
more. Prices and availablility subject to change.